The Rise and Fall
of the House of Windsor

A. N. WILSON

The Rise and Fall of the House of Windsor

Fawcett Columbine • New York

A Fawcett Columbine Book
Published by Ballantine Books

Copyright © 1993, 1994 by A. N. Wilson

All rights reserved under International and Pan-American Copyright
Conventions. Published in the United States by Ballantine Books,
a division of Random House, Inc., New York.

This edition published by arrangement with
W. W. Norton & Company, Inc.

The author and publisher wish to thank the following for use of
photographs: 1b, 2b, 4a, 6b, 7, 9, 11a, 12a, The Camera Press; 12b, 15, 16,
Tim Graham; 1a, 5, The National Portrait Gallery; 8, 11b, Popperfoto;
14, Rex Features; 2a, 3, 4b, 6a, 10, Topham Picture Source.

Library of Congress Catalog Card Number: 93-91052

ISBN: 0-449-90932-8

Cover design by Susan Grube
Cover photo of Buckingham Palace © John Scowen/FPG International

Manufactured in the United States of America

First Ballantine Books Edition: June 1994

10 9 8 7 6 5 4 3 2 1

Contents

The House of Windsor

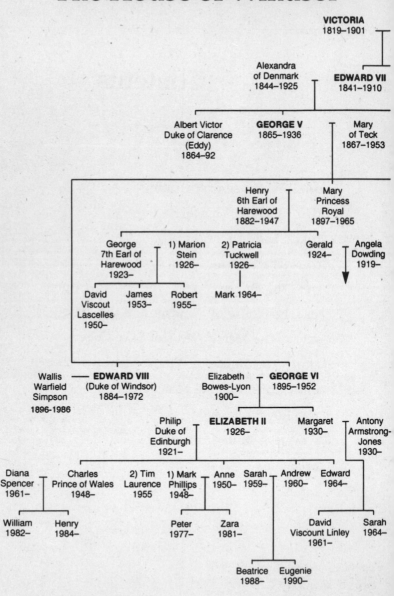

VICTORIA
1819–1901

Alexandra
of Denmark
1844–1925

EDWARD VII
1841–1910

Albert Victor
Duke of Clarence
(Eddy)
1864–92

GEORGE V
1865–1936

Mary
of Teck
1867–1953

Henry
6th Earl of
Harewood
1882–1947

Mary
Princess
Royal
1897–1965

George
7th Earl of
Harewood
1923–

1) Marion
Stein
1926–

2) Patricia
Tuckwell
1926–

Gerald
1924–

Angela
Dowding
1919–

David
Viscout
Lascelles
1950–

James
1953–

Robert
1955–

Mark 1964–

Wallis
Warfield
Simpson
1896-1986

EDWARD VIII
(Duke of Windsor)
1884–1972

Elizabeth
Bowes-Lyon
1900–

GEORGE VI
1895–1952

Philip
Duke of
Edinburgh
1921–

ELIZABETH II
1926–

Margaret
1930–

Antony
Armstrong-
Jones
1930–

Diana
Spencer
1961–

Charles
Prince of Wales
1948–

2) Tim
Laurence
1955

1) Mark
Phillips
1948–

Anne
1950–

Sarah
1959–

Andrew
1960–

Edward
1964–

William
1982–

Henry
1984–

Peter
1977–

Zara
1981–

David
Viscount Linley
1961–

Sarah
1964–

Beatrice
1988–

Eugenie
1990–

The House of Windsor

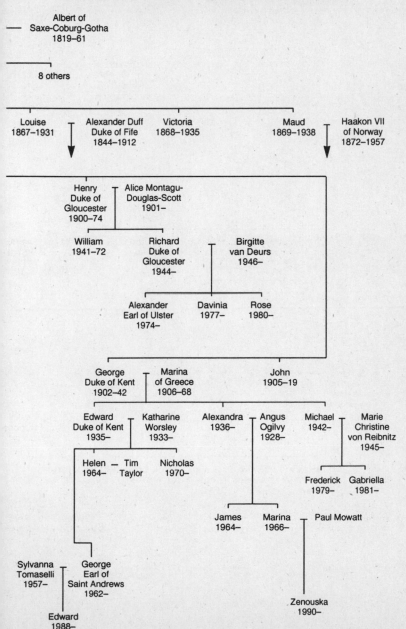

Albert of
Saxe-Coburg-Gotha
1819–61

8 others

Louise
1867–1931

Alexander Duff
Duke of Fife
1844–1912

Victoria
1868–1935

Maud
1869–1938

Haakon VII
of Norway
1872–1957

Henry
Duke of
Gloucester
1900–74

Alice Montagu-
Douglas-Scott
1901–

William
1941–72

Richard
Duke of
Gloucester
1944–

Birgitte
van Deurs
1946–

Alexander
Earl of Ulster
1974–

Davinia
1977–

Rose
1980–

George
Duke of Kent
1902–42

Marina
of Greece
1906–68

John
1905–19

Edward
Duke of Kent
1935–

Katharine
Worsley
1933–

Alexandra
1936–

Angus
Ogilvy
1928–

Michael
1942–

Marie
Christine
von Reibnitz
1945–

Helen — Tim
1964–   Taylor

Nicholas
1970–

Frederick
1979–

Gabriella
1981–

James
1964–

Marina
1966–

Paul Mowatt

Sylvanna
Tomaselli
1957–

George
Earl of
Saint Andrews
1962–

Zenouska
1990–

Edward
1988–

ONE

The Curse
of the Coburgs

'I know this sounds crazy, but I've lived before.'

Lady Diana Spencer
on the 'Squidgygate' tapes

'Then verily shall I pray to the Lord Almighty to
visit the sins of the fathers upon the children to
the third and fourth generation of the Coburg line.'

Brother Emericus Kohary

On November 23, 1992, speaking at a banquet to celebrate forty years on the throne and forty-five years of her marriage, Queen Elizabeth II admitted that the previous twelve months had been an *annus horribilis*. Three days before, her childhood home, Windsor Castle, had suffered a major fire. But this was only one of the calamities to befall the British Royal Family in this disastrous year. The Royal Family's claim, until recently, had always been that it represented an ideal of family stability to which the British people could look for an example of Christian home life. In March, Prince Andrew, the Queen's favourite son, announced that his marriage to Sarah Ferguson was over. A few months later, his sister had divorced her husband, Captain Mark Phillips. By the end of the year, 'Fergie', otherwise known as Her Royal Highness the Duchess of York, had been photographed in the South of France having her toes sucked by a 'financial adviser' from Texas; Charles and Diana had announced their separation; the Queen had been forced to pay income tax; and, even in the most conservative quarters, the unthinkable question was being asked: could the Monarchy survive?

No one could doubt that the Royal Family, as individuals, had had a bad year – three marital separations and a major fire is more than most families have to endure in a single twelve-month period. But does this mean that there is actually a crisis in the institution of the Monarchy itself? No one could fail to see that there had been a change in the Monarchy's relations with the Press during the forty years that Queen Elizabeth II had been on the throne. At the beginning of this period, there were many conventions governing the way in which journalists spoke of royalties; little by little, these conventions (which were, in any case, of very recent vintage) began to be discarded, not only by newspapers but by the royalties themselves. In 1953, it was 'not done' to repeat what was said to you by a Royal Personage, let alone reprint it in the newspapers. By 1992, members of the Royal Family were themselves 'leaking' the most intimate details of their private lives to the Press.

The relations between the Royal Family and the Press are of obvious importance: without the Press and television, how would any of us know about these people? And there can be no doubt that there have been many crises in the relations between these two institutions which feed off, and to a large degree encourage, one another.

These 'crises', or scoops, depending on your point of view, can be exciting for a few days. When the Duchess of York was photographed in the South of France, everyone might have deplored the intrusion into her privacy. It would, however, have been an austere figure who would not have turned the pages of *Paris-Match* or the *Daily Mirror* during that week, had the opportunity to do so arisen. By a similar token, most people have enjoyed reading the transcripts of a telephone conversation in which the Prince of Wales declared that he would like to be reincarnated as Mrs Parker-Bowles's Tampax, just as, some months earlier, they enjoyed accounts of his wife being sick and having tantrums. One does not have to be of a very vindictive temperament to savour the essentially comic misfortunes of a talentless and, it has to be said at the outset, largely charmless family who, by the accidents of birth and marriage, happen to be the custodians of the British monarchical system. It is they who have chosen to behave like characters in a Feydeau farce, and they cannot be surprised when the audience laugh. Figures such as the Princess Royal who have not chosen to tell the newspapers about their marital secrets, have been highly esteemed. (In Princess Anne's case, while her abrasive manner might have been noticed from time to time, she is largely regarded as a sportswoman and charity organiser: rumours about her private life, in general circulation among journalists, never, to my knowledge, saw print.)

Entertaining as the Feydeau-esque interludes might be, it remains to be seen whether they are damaging to the institution of Monarchy as such. Journalists like to believe that they have power and influence, and so it is not surprising that they should declare that such incidents as the Royal toe-sucking or the Royal Tampax pose 'serious constitutional questions'. In the seemingly interminable journalistic debates about the subject, there has been an interesting class division, perhaps because the British always try to resolve questions of politics or religion by reference to class.

Andrew Neil, the Editor of the *Sunday Times*, which first published extracts from the book *Diana: Her True Story*, is a lower-middle-class Scot. He believes that the institution of Monarchy should go or be changed, and while he is about it he would like to shake up all the snobs and toffs who run what he believes to be the Establishment in Britain today. There probably still is an Establishment, and it probably bears some hazy resemblance to the Establishment of Mr Neil's worst nightmares, but it has not been this 'Establishment' which has responded to him. Rather, it has been the more middle-class, public-school-educated of his fellow-journalists who have enjoyed baiting him by adopting a pro-monarchical position.

At the right-wing extreme there have been High Tory journalists with an aristocratic point of view who believe that the country has now become unworthy of the Monarchy. Sir Peregrine Worsthorne, the Highest Tory of them all, as well as being the noblest and most aristocratic journalist at work in Britain today, has proposed that republicanism is the only true faith that a monarchist can now adopt. The almost equally aristocratic Mr Auberon Waugh, who for years in his journalism has excoriated and insulted members of the Royal Family, was turned by the indiscretions of the Princess of Wales in the *Sunday Times* into an adherent (more or less) of the Worsthorne school, believing that the classless New Brits, as he calls them, have become entirely unworthy of our excellent Royal Family. 'The Windsors have served this country well,' he now writes (though you would not have guessed it to read his journalism for the last quarter-century); his advice is 'that they should be allowed to return to Germany with dignity and decorum, the plaudits of a grateful people ringing in their ears, and leave Princess Monster* behind on her own to receive the cheers of her adulatory fans,

* Mr Waugh's unkind way of referring to HRH the Princess of Wales, *vide Spectator*, January 30, 1993.

Madonna-like, until they grow bored and decide to tear her to pieces'.

Behind such journalistic rough-and-tumble, there exists one possible reason for believing that the Royal House of Windsor is in difficulties. That is, that Britain has changed so much since the Queen's Coronation that it is in some way no longer appropriate for it to be governed by a monarch and by a system which is inherently monarchical – a non-elective Second Chamber in Parliament, a system of patronage extending to many areas of public life, in the Armed Forces and the Civil Service, and an established Church. No political institution survives if it is not flexible in the face of change, and one of the reasons that the British Monarchy survived so comparatively vigorously after the First World War, when so many other European dynasties collapsed, was, precisely, its constitutional flexibility.

But equally, no institution, political, religious or social, can survive if it has no function, and if the conditions in which it flourished have altered so fundamentally that it has nothing to sustain it.

This book is an attempt to examine whether the House of Windsor – and with it the British Monarchy – is indeed in a state of crisis. I shall examine various aspects of the Crown's function – its relations with the Press, its symbolic role as a guardian of pure home life and monogamy, its traditional Christian function, embodied in the Queen's claim to be Defender of the Faith, and its constitutional role. In the first three areas, I believe that the Royal Family are in desperate trouble. Their relations with the Press have been disastrous; their claim to be symbols of a Christian happy family look, to say the least, hollow in the light of their real marital history; and the Sovereign's role as Supreme Governor of the National Church appears harder and harder to sustain, for two powerful reasons: most English people are not Anglicans, and most Anglicans do not want their unique status as an Established religion to continue.

It is in the fourth, and most crucial, area – the constitutional area – that I believe the Monarchy to be much stronger than the journalists would have us suppose. When the British (Old Brits as well as New Brits, I fear) have all finished laughing at the Royal Family in the newspapers; and when they have reflected how few of them – less than two-and-a-half per cent – share their Sovereign's religious faith, there remains an overwhelming majority of British people who wish the Monarchy to continue. This is not merely for sentimental reasons, important as those are: it is because they dislike the idea of an elective presidential system. In the years which follow, there will indubitably be calls by British politicians to have such a system, not least because some British politicians would no doubt like to be President themselves. As Britain moves towards closer and closer political as well as economic union with the other European nations, it will seem advisable to some of the keener 'Europeans' that Britain should have an elected president, like the Italians, the French and the Germans. This is not an argument which will be easily won, however, when the British remind themselves of the constitutional history of those three countries in the last sixty years.

The House of Windsor is not composed of interesting people: few of them, except the Queen herself, are even very remarkable. From 1936 to the present time, they would seem to be able to capture the public imagination only when dying or committing adultery. Their dullness might make them unappealing to newspapers, but it might be a large part of their political strength. For the paradox is that the British Monarchy has actually gained in political strength and importance during the reign of Queen Elizabeth II, though this partly has to do with the popular reaction against Margaret Thatcher and the phenomenon known as Thatcherism.

Before tackling my four great issues, therefore – the Press, Royal marriages, religion and the Constitution – it will be necessary to assess the recent history of the House of Windsor, and I have chosen to do so not in a strictly chronological framework but by sketching very briefly the *dramatis personae*. There are, I think, four crucially important figures in this story: Margaret Thatcher, Lady Diana Spencer, Prince Charles and Queen Elizabeth II, and it would not be possible to discuss the generalities without paying some attention at first to these particular individuals. Only when we have done so can we decide whether there is a future for the House of Windsor, or whether the noise of tumbrils is soon to be heard on the cobblestones of the stable courtyards of Buckingham Palace.

Before that, however, we must remind ourselves that the House of Windsor is not really 'of Windsor' at all. During the First World War, the British were embarrassed by the fact that their Sovereign, though speaking like a Cockney and dressing like a minor English country squire, should be of purely Germanic origin. 'I may be uninspiring,' King George V remarked, 'but I'll be damned if I'm an alien.' Like many persons of foreign origin who have settled in Britain, he decided to change the family name to something impeccably British. The House of Saxe-Coburg-Gotha (as the Royal Family has been called since Queen Victoria married Prince Albert of Saxe-Coburg) would be renamed the House of Windsor.

'The true royal tradition died on that day in 1917 when, for a mere war, King George V changed his name,' said the distinguished Bavarian nobleman Count Albrecht von

Montgelas. The Kaiser, more good-humouredly, asked if he could attend a performance of *The Merry Wives of Saxe-Coburg-Gotha*.*

What is perhaps less generally discussed is the Royal Family's entitlement even to the Saxe-Coburg inheritance. This would perhaps be of interest only to pedantic genealogists, were it not for the curious story of the Curse of the Coburgs.

Both Albert and Victoria came of the Coburg line. Albert's father was the brother of Victoria's mother (the Duchess of Kent). Their brother, Ferdinand, married Antoinette de Kohary, the only child of Prince Joseph Kohary, Chancellor to the Austrian Emperor and a member of one of the richest families in Hungary. The Coburg estate was entailed in favour of the male line, but Prince Joseph persuaded the Emperor to issue a 'filiation' order, which bestowed on Antoinette the benefits of a son. The male members of the Kohary family resisted in vain, and one of them, the monk Brother Emericus Kohary, went to a churchyard in Darmstadt at midnight and solemnly read out the curse according to the ritual of the *Manuale Exorcisorum*.† 'Then verily shall I pray to the Lord Almighty to visit the sins of the fathers upon the children to the third and fourth generation of the Coburg line.'

The efficacy of this malediction may be assessed if we pause to follow the Coburg line through the four prescribed generations and see how they fared. One could fill a book with the names of the descendants of the House of Saxe-Coburg, which was in effect the nursery for most of the Royal Families of Europe in the nineteenth century. But, even allowing for the selectivity of the following account,

---

* Kenneth Rose, *King George V* (1983) p.174.
† David Duff, *Hessian Tapestry* (1967) p. 46.

which traces only the more immediate relations of the present Duke of Edinburgh, the reader will feel compelled to acknowledge that the breed has been singularly unfortunate since the monk uttered his curse.

In the first generation, Prince Albert died of typhoid fever at the age of only forty-two. His wife and cousin, Victoria, had unknowingly inherited haemophilia from her Coburg mother, also called Victoria, and therefore passed on this fatal disease (which is 'carried' on the X chromosome and therefore can be borne quite unconsciously by females) to the Royal Families of Spain, Bulgaria, Greece, Germany and Russia. The Portuguese Royal Family, also inheritors of the Coburg line and of the monk's curse, were almost entirely wiped out by the same disease which killed Prince Albert, typhoid fever.

But let us limit our pursuit to the line which eventually produces Prince Philip. The next generation – the second generation of the monk's curse – is that of Princess Alice, who married Louis IV, Grand Duke of Hesse and the Rhine, in 1862. Like her father, she was destined to die young (only thirty-five) of diphtheria, caught from the lips of a dying infant daughter. She did not die, however, before producing a good crop of children, all of whose lives would have surely gratified the malicious Kohary monk, had he lived to witness them. Most famous of them was Alix (Aleksandra Feodorovna), last of the Tsarinas, who perished with her husband, Tsar Nicholas II, and all her children at the hands of the Bolsheviks at Ekaterinaburg in 1918. Her sister, Ella Feodorovna, a Grand Duchess of Russia, also died at the hands of the Bolsheviks – she was thrown live down a mineshaft at Alapevsk in Siberia, her husband having been assassinated in Red Square thirteen years before, during the Russo-Japanese war. Their other siblings included Frederick ('Frittie'), who died at the age of three by falling out of his mother's bedroom window (not before his haemophilia had been diagnosed), and their sister little Princess Marie, who died of the black diphtheria which also killed her mother. There was also Princess Victoria of Hesse and the Rhine, who in 1884 married Louis Prince of Battenberg, who changed his name to Mountbatten in the same year, 1917, that George V changed the Royal House to that of Windsor and was granted the reassuringly British-sounding title Marquess of Milford Haven. The former Princess Victoria of Battenberg, later the Marchioness of Milford Haven, Prince Philip's grandmother, lived to see the birth of her great-grandchildren, Prince Charles and Princess Anne, before dying in 1950. It might therefore be supposed that she had bypassed the curse of the monk.

But presumably, for a curse to be fully satisfying to the malice of its perpetrator, there must be some unfortunates who survive in order to witness the calamities and misfortunes befalling its most direct victims. The Marchioness of Milford Haven lived long enough to see the disastrously unhappy marriage of her daughter Alice (mother of Prince Philip) to Andrew, Prince of Greece and Denmark. She also witnessed one of the most extraordinary consequences of the monk's malice, which wiped out most of the adolescent Prince Philip's relations at a stroke and which left a permanent scar on his nature. In 1937, Prince Louis of Hesse announced his engagement to the Hon. Margaret Campbell-Geddes; the wedding was to be held in England. Prince Philip of Greece, aged sixteen, went down to London for the wedding, and awaited the arrival of his Hesse relations at Croydon airport. November 16 was a clear sunny day as their aeroplane took off from the Continent, and it was only when they approached Croydon that a freak mist gathered. The plane crashed into a chimney and was smashed to pieces. All the crown jewels were lost, as were many members of the family – Hereditary Grand Duke George Donatus, his wife, his two young sons, Louis and Alexander, the Dowager Grand Duchess Eleonore, and so forth.* Only the baby of the family, Johanna, was left behind. She died of tubercular meningitis two years later, aged three. Some weeks later, while Prince Philip was still reeling from the shock of this multiple bereavement, his favourite sister Cecile was killed in another air crash, this time over Brussels, aged twenty-six.

The Kohary monk extended his curse to the 'third and fourth generation' of the Coburg line. If we take it that Victoria and Albert were the first generation, then the fourth (limiting our studies specifically to the direct ancestors of Prince Philip) comes to an end with his mother, Princess Alice, a melancholic nun who was to be seen drifting sadly about the corridors of Buckingham Palace dressed in her religious habit. Perhaps her piety and prayers were offered in reparation for the Curse of the Coburgs. If so, they could not prevent the monk's little *coup de grâce*, the assassination of her brother, Earl Mountbatten of Burma, in the summer of 1976 on a yacht off the coast of Ireland.

It might be supposed, as readily as it is to be hoped, that the curse of the Kohary monk has now spent its force. The four generations specified in his ritual commination have now been born, and even those who are unable to believe in such things on rational grounds must concede

---

* The young couple were married wearing full mourning, with Lord Mountbatten as best man and Von Ribbentrop, the German Ambassador in London, signing the register. Princess Margaret Mountbatten (the former Miss Campbell-Geddes) returned to Germany with her young husband and five coffins. 'Everybody was crying,' she recalled, 'even when they were doing the Nazi salute, they were still crying.' Tim Heald, *The Duke. A Portrait of Prince Philip* (1991) p.49.

that, since the churchyard utterance, the descendants of the House of Coburg have had immoderate ill fortune.

Some will have wondered, when they read – or heard – the claim by the Princess of Wales that she had 'lived before', whether by some cruel quirk of destiny she had walked the earth before in the person of the Kohary monk, and whether, in her falling-out with her husband, she threatened to undermine what had appeared, until she married Prince Charles, to be an institution of unshakeable durability. Others will dismiss all talk of curses or reincarnation as mere fantasy: but they will think that monarchs, like maledictory monks, belong to a vanished age. To such as these, the march of historical change is not to be resisted.

The gradual dissolution of the class structures in modern Britain and the undermining of its Parliamentary sovereignty and independence by European federalism perhaps make the notion of a constitutional Monarch seem a trifle anachronistic. In time, and given a crisis – so such forward-looking minds would conceive – the House of Windsor will have to go. Just as the huge proportion of their cousins among the royalties and high nobilities of Old Europe have been swept away by history, so, it is imagined, will they. If France elects a President and Germany elects a President – why shouldn't Great Britain? In which case, without the violence which disposed of their cousin the Tsar, the House of Windsor might – like so many of their German cousins – retreat to their large houses and their obscure lives, and allow history to march on without them.

Those who believe this moment of history to have arrived are still very much in the minority in Britain, but they have gathered in numbers and momentum. Even a decade ago, the only British people who regarded themselves as republicans were almost all recognisable eccentrics – the sort of people who would also believe in reforming the English spelling system, or who would doubt the authorship of Shakespeare's plays. Something happened during the 1980s which changed all that. A carefully thought republicanism is still a minority fad in Britain, but it has gained ground and *gravitas*. And one of the people responsible for that is the woman who cast her personality so forcefully on the decade between 1979 and 1989: the Right Honourable Margaret Thatcher.

TWO

Margaret Thatcher's Legacy

'We have enjoyed ourselves immensely.'

Margaret Thatcher
in the Soviet Union

The removal of Margaret Thatcher from political office, after nearly eleven years as the Prime Minister of Great Britain, was accomplished with remarkably little fuss. Once it had happened, it was accepted on all sides with a certain degree of incredulity. For many people in the world – Russians, Americans, Japanese, Europeans of the EC and of the former Warsaw Pact (perhaps particularly for this category) – it was simply incomprehensible that the British Conservative party should have chosen to remove from power a leader of such outstanding qualities. Mrs Thatcher had been more than a politician, she had been an icon. Wherever she went in the world, she was recognised and – a scarcely English phenomenon – what she stood for was recognised. This was particularly marked in her visits to Eastern Europe. Her early expression of confidence that she could 'do business' with Mikhail Gorbachov meant that she believed that she could abolish world communism. Together with her political ally and close personal friend President Ronald Reagan of the United States, she believed herself to have done this, and she spoke openly of the part she had played in *glasnost*, the collapse of the Berlin Wall and the gradual undoing of Soviet power. Her 'values' – a belief in self-determination, in personal freedom, in a reduction of State interference and the promotion of *laissez-faire* economics, a hatred of left-wing tyrannies, a willingness to 'do business' with right-wing tyrannies (most notably in South Africa), and an uncomplicated belief in Bible Christianity – all seemed much more American than British, which is one of the reasons for her continued and immense popularity in the United States.

At home in Britain, the picture was rather different. A small number of right-wing ideologues rejoiced in her as a revolutionary who had reversed (as they hoped, for ever) the march of the liberal consensus. A much larger group – the electorate who returned her to office in three successive general elections – saw, like the rest of the world, that she 'stood for' things, and they were things which they liked. She was unashamedly belligerent in her attitude to foreigners. When General Galtieri invaded the Malvinas in 1981, she immediately sent a task force of British servicemen to boot him out again. Liberals watched askance, but this action won her enormous popularity, not merely with the vulgar newspapers ('GOTCHA!' said the headline of the *Sun* newspaper on the morning the Argentinian ship the *Belgrano* was sunk by Her Majesty's Navy) but with the electorate at large. So did her clever trick of persuading the electorate that under her they paid less tax. (In fact they paid more, but she reduced direct taxation and increased indirect, thereby greatly benefiting the New Rich and increasing the gap between rich and poor.)

According to the Thatcherite way of viewing history, Britain, which had been a bumbling, decaying little island, controlled first by an Aristocratic Oligarchy (1689–1939), then by a Government of National Unity (1939–1945), then by a Socialist Experiment (1945–1951), and at last by the Liberal Consensus which was the heir to the Whig Consensus of Aristocratic times (1951–1979), suddenly found itself proclaimed as a 'share-owning, property-owning democracy'. Those who were unable to afford to do so were encouraged to take out mortgages and buy their own homes. Nationalised industries were sold off, and a high proportion of the holdings were sold to small private investors. The Trades Unions, most notably the National Union of Mineworkers, who were seen to have held the country 'to ransom' for forty or fifty years, were seen off with crippling legislation and an even more crippling miners' strike, which the miners lost and which weakened British manufacturing industry, particularly in the North.

There could be no doubt, in the shared minds of Mrs Thatcher and her supporters in the popular right-wing press, of who was in charge. Everyone knew, when they considered the matter rationally, that Mrs Thatcher was not really 'in charge' any more than any previous Prime Minister had been. The economy was still, in fact, controlled by forces over which Government had very limited power. The European Community, in spite of Mrs Thatcher's rudeness to the French and Belgians and Germans when she went abroad, continued to extend its influence; and when she was presented with legislation such as the Single European Act, Mrs Thatcher signed up to it without a murmur. Educational standards, on which as Minister of Education Mrs Thatcher had appeared to set such store (she abolished nearly twice as many grammar schools as her socialist predecessor Mrs Williams), continued to decline catastrophically, and the crime rate soared. What was more, Mrs Thatcher was the least 'Thatcherite' Prime Minister when it came to public spending, which she increased with liberal gusto every year she was in office – on transport, defence, the police, on health and social services.

The reality, however, was far less important than the propaganda; and nearly everyone believed in a part of themselves that this little woman, with her firm blonde hair-do, and her handbag, and her dark blue and white suits, was a Leader such as Britain had never known in peacetime. This was particularly true of the Opposition parties, Liberal and Labour, who attributed nearly all the evils of the age – increasing crime and unemployment, a tendency towards British isolationism in Europe, etcetera – less to the general policies of the Conservative Party than to the personal will of Mrs Thatcher. In consequence, when they went to the polls and tried to persuade the electorate to return a Liberal Government or a Labour Government, the electorate voted for the little woman with the handbag. Far from being an electoral liability as her enemies within the Conservative Party claimed, she had a genius for winning elections.

Margaret Thatcher had pulled off the trick – achieved in the past by Bismarck, among other great political leaders – of appearing on one level to be quite independent of her party or movement. While in any poll only forty per cent of the electorate thought the Conservatives were a worthy party of Government, eighty to ninety per cent believed that Margaret Thatcher was not merely the most eligible Prime Minister, but, little by little, the natural Prime Minister. She was in 'a class of her own', and it was imaginatively impossible to replace her.

On this irrational, gut level, Mrs Thatcher had become

something much more than the Prime Minister, and certainly much more than the Parliamentary Leader of the Conservatives. She had become a grand national icon, frequently depicted by cartoonists as Britannia, the emblem of Britain itself. On one level she had achieved presidential, almost monarchical, status.

Relations between Mrs Thatcher and that other little woman with a handbag, Her Majesty Queen Elizabeth II of Great Britain and Northern Ireland and her dominions beyond the seas, were known to be frosty, if not positively glacial. The Queen is known to favour the 'Liberal consensus' by which Great Britain was governed throughout the first thirty years of her reign. She had famously enjoyed harmonious relations with all her previous Prime Ministers. After Sir Winston Churchill there had been that firebrand Whig Anthony Eden, followed by the Whig of Whigs, Harold Macmillan. (Throughout this period, incidentally, the Labour Party had decided that they disliked the socialist experiment of 1945–50 as much as the British electorate had done, and they had elected as their leader Mr Gaitskell, who in all important areas – defence and public spending – thought roughly the same as the Conservatives.) The collapse of Sir Alec Douglas-Home's Government of 1963–4 meant that the Whig Consensus had to be dressed up in slightly more plebeian clothes. Harold Wilson and Edward Heath became successive Prime Ministers, speaking with plebeian accents and boasting of their low social origins, but both fundamentally upholders of the old status quo – the power of the Civil Service, the power of the Foreign Office in foreign affairs, a Keynesian economic outlook, a generous view of social services. No wonder the Queen had liked them all, for these were all policies in which she had been brought up to believe, and, much more importantly, they were the policies which underpinned the Monarchy.

The British Monarchy since 1689 has had a peculiarly bloodless history when compared with the other Royal Houses of Europe. This is because, after James II was forced from his throne in 1688 by the Whigs, it has always been perfectly apparent who actually exercised power in Britain. Kings and Queens only need to have their heads chopped off when they exercise power – as happened to James II's father, Charles I. The Hanoverian compromise after the death of James II's last surviving sister, Anne, in 1702, was for the ruling upper class to put in a monarch of their own choosing, and this was done when they found the Elector of Hanover, an obese divorced German who knew almost no English, and proclaimed him as George I. Ever since then, the British Monarchs have known who called the tune, and, with the defeat of any attempts to put the 'rightful' Stuart Monarch on the throne (the so-called Jacobite rebellions of 1715 and 1745), something stronger than mere alliance grew up between the British Monarch and the governing class. It was symbiosis; the one fed the other, was dependent on the other for its life.

So while all real power was exercised by the governing class – who returned the Members of Parliament from their pocket boroughs, and formed Cabinets and elected Prime Ministers largely from the Upper House, the House of Lords – the ultimate sanction for this power rested, technically speaking, with the Crown. This had an extraordinarily stabilising effect throughout the nineteenth century, when other European countries were convulsed with revolutions and counter-revolutions. The gradual extension of franchise – first in 1831 and 1832 with the Great Reform Bill, leading inexorably much later in the century (with the Reform Act of 1867) to the possibility of 'universal suffrage', that is, 'one man, one vote', then in the twentieth century to votes for men and women over the age of majority – all happened not merely with the Monarch's consent but, crucially, with the Monarch's involvement. No one believed that William IV would have been able to stop the Reform Bill of 1831; but his involvement (and he was no political genius) did actually ensure the passage of the Bill without a threat to the status quo. A very similar thing happened in 1910, shortly after the accession of George V, when the 'left wing' of the Liberal Party threatened to create 500 peers to force through the abolition of the House of Lords unless Lloyd George's radical Budget was accepted. George V was able to intervene and save the situation in rather the same way that William IV, another dim-witted sailor king, had intervened in 1831. When it came to the point of decision, the governing class did not want to lose the Monarchy any more than the Monarchy wished to lose the governing class. As the governing class changed, the Monarchy adapted, but both continued to depend upon one another until the arrival of Margaret Thatcher.

In all her public pronouncements about the Queen, in particular since her own fall from grace, Margaret Thatcher has been deferential to the point of oiliness. This hardly disguises the fact that, throughout her years in office, the Queen and Mrs Thatcher were perceived as being not merely at odds over individual political questions, but also in a sense rivals for the same job. Almost the only area of public debate where the Queen has allowed her personal views to be known is in the future of the British Commonwealth.

It is possible that the Queen is the only person in the British Isles who is interested in the British Commonwealth. Most of her subjects have some difficulty in remembering what exactly it is. The Commonwealth is sometimes described by Her Majesty as 'a family of nations', the nations in question being those which used to comprise the former British Empire. For someone whose mother was the last, self-styled, Empress of India, it is hardly surprising that the Queen should have grown up with a strong sense of her Imperial responsibilities. The wireless broadcast which she made as Princess Elizabeth, on her twenty-first birthday, was not to the nation but to the Empire. It was delivered not from London but from Cape Town.

She told her Imperial father's subjects that she saw her coming-of-age as a self-dedication. 'I should like to make that dedication now. It is very simple. I declare before you that my whole life, whether it be long or short, shall be devoted to your service and the service of our great Imperial Commonwealth to which we all belong. But I shall not have strength to carry out this resolution unless you join in it with me, as I now invite you to do; I know that your support will be unfailingly given. God bless all of you who are willing to share it.'

These words, spoken on April 21, 1947, were sincerely meant at the time, and the Queen has gone on sincerely meaning them, long after the political reality to which they referred – Great Britain an Imperial power in the world – has evaporated. The unity of the Commonwealth is always something upon which Her Majesty has set much store, and successive British Prime Ministers have paid lip-service to this idea, largely for reasons of politeness, and have entertained the Commonwealth leaders to annual dinners and functions. Whenever the leaders sat down together to discuss politics, there were clashes and disagreements, since they did not in fact represent any cohesive entity beyond the fact that, historically, their countries were all former British dominions or dependencies. This was never more sharply apparent than in the attitude of the British Commonwealth Conference to the country where Princess Elizabeth first made her moving self-dedication:

South Africa.

Well trained in the art of political flannel, and believing the liberal consensus to be almost as sacred as her Coronation Oath, Her Majesty very naturally sided with the Commonwealth leaders in their desire to impose economic sanctions on South Africa (an ex-member of the Commonwealth!) as a means of putting pressure on the all-white Government to abolish the apartheid laws.

Mrs Thatcher took a notoriously different view, and stood up to the various Commonwealth leaders with characteristic robustness. When accused of the immorality of not imposing sanctions on South Africa, she said, 'I find nothing moral about people sitting in comfortable circumstances, with good salaries, inflation-proof pensions, good jobs, saying that we, as a matter of morality, will put x hundred thousand black people out of work, knowing that this could lead to starvation, poverty, unemployment, and even greater violence.'

It was at the Commonwealth Conference of 1986 that these issues were to be debated by the different nations who attended. Two days before the opening of the conference, the *Sunday Times* claimed that there was now a breach between Margaret Thatcher and her Sovereign.* Most of the story was subsequently admitted by the editor of that newspaper to be untrue. It had claimed that the Queen differed from Margaret Thatcher over a whole range of issues, ranging from the Libyan bombings to the miners' strike and the poverty of the inner cities. Their 'clash' over Africa was merely the latest example of the Queen being 'worried to the point of outrage' by the Iron Lady.

There had been plenty of occasions in history where Prime Ministers and their sovereigns had had personal

* July 20, 1986.

disagreements: Gladstone disapproved of Queen Victoria's attitude towards the Ottoman Empire, for example; George V disliked Lloyd George's Bismarckian Social Welfare schemes; there were clashes, particularly in the early days, between Winston Churchill and George VI. What was entirely new in the disagreement between Mrs Thatcher and the Queen* was its public nature. The *Sunday Times* article, like so much journalism, was an example of something where 'everything was true except the facts'. While it was obviously untrue that the Queen wished to express her views about the Prime Minister by 'leaking' them to one of Mr Rupert Murdoch's newspapers, there was a perceptible public difference of style between the two women. While there was no reason to suppose that they did not conduct themselves with perfect politeness at their weekly meetings, there was no secret made by the Prime Minister that she thought such encounters 'a waste of time'. And over the African question, they plainly did take different sides – the Queen holding the view that the Commonwealth must be held together at all costs, and Margaret Thatcher regarding the Commonwealth with increasing impatience.

The *Sunday Times* article, inaccurate as it was in substance, was believed, and this was a symptom of the fact that the British public thought of Margaret Thatcher and the Queen as rivals.

This was understandable, given the fact that Mrs Thatcher appeared, as time went on, to adopt a manner which was increasingly regal. Her adoption of the royal

---

* Or 'Buckingham Palace', as the Queen is usually called on such occasions. Throughout her *annus horribilis*, it was noticeable that whenever the Queen expressed disgust, astonishment, disagreement or outrage with her subjects she was referred to as if she were this substantial work of architecture. ('Buckingham Palace said last night that . . .') When things go right, the Queen is referred to in her own person.

'we' in her speech was only a symptom of this. 'We are a grandmother', said to the waiting reporters after the birth of a son to her son Mark and his wife, is the most famous of these utterances. The biographers include many other examples: 'We are in the fortunate position in Britain, of being, as it were, the senior person in power.' And again – having visited some block of flats in Moscow – 'We have enjoyed ourselves immensely.'

Whether, at the height of her power, Mrs Thatcher regarded herself as regal, we shall have to wait for history to decide. Certainly she more and more took upon herself roles which had traditionally been fulfilled by royalties, rather than by politicians. The Queen is a naturally diffident person, and when disasters occur, she is frightened that her immediate appearance on the scene to comfort the survivors will distract the rescue-workers, nurses and such people from the job they are wishing to do. 'I shall only be in the way,' she is quoted as saying.* Nevertheless, she has been unobtrusively faithful in turning up at scenes of calamity to offer comfort to those left behind; it was a tradition which went back to the Second World War, when the Queen's father, King George VI, and her mother, Queen Elizabeth, were tireless in visiting bomb-sites and hospitals. The only peacetime occasion on which the Queen has deliberately stayed away from a disaster, delaying her visit by a few days – Aberfan, where a slagheap collapsed on a primary school, killing many of the children in the Welsh mining village in October 1966 – is privately regarded by Her Majesty as the greatest mistake of her reign.†

It was noticed by the Royal Family that the longer the

* Douglas Keay, *Elizabeth II* (1991), p.256.

† Douglas Keay, p.247.

Prime Minister was in office, the more she seemed to be taking upon herself this role of the national figurehead. In the spring of 1987 a British cross-Channel ferry sank outside the Belgian port of Zeebrugge. Mrs Thatcher set out at once, but not before telling her staff that the Palace presence – in this case the Duke and Duchess of York – was not to be allowed to upstage her own. If this story by Hugo Young* is true (and there is no particular reason to doubt it), it implies that by this stage of her Premiership Mrs Thatcher had risen above the rule that Prime Ministers do not travel abroad without the consent or at least the knowledge of the Monarch, since she rapidly flew off to Belgium.

While Mrs Thatcher was still Prime Minister, most people in Britain felt that they had more to think about than her effect on the Royal Family. As the country lurched from one drama to the next – now a war, now a great national strike, now an artificially created boom which gave everyone the impression that their homes had doubled in value (by which they meant that their houses had doubled in price) – the Queen was not to the forefront of anyone's attention. It was only after Mrs Thatcher's removal from office by the *coup d'état* of 1990 that the British people began to absorb the imaginative effect of her years of power and to sense that one of her legacies has been a weakening of the importance of the Monarchy. Those who disliked Mrs Thatcher helped to create this impression even more strongly than those who cheered on 'the Leaderene', and this is for two very simple reasons.

The first is that everyone felt that they had passed through more than a decade of all but monarchy in the reign of Margaret. With her upstaging of the Royal Family themselves, her use of the royal 'we' to describe herself,

* *One of Us*, (1990) p.492.

her immense appeal at election time, her genius in front of television and film cameras, Margaret Thatcher had begun to displace the Queen and to demonstrate that the British could have a very plausible national leader who was not a Monarch but an elected representative.

The second anti-monarchical legacy of Mrs Thatcher is that she is a democrat. It is not exactly clear at what stage of her career she became one, but there can be no doubt of her democratic credentials now that she has been released from the shackles of power. Her objections to the British ratification of the Maastricht Treaty have taken a singularly democratic turn for one who, in the days of her power, rejected any notion of a referendum as a way of determining the destiny of events. Because all three major political parties in Britain support the Treaty, Lady Thatcher takes the democratic view that Parliament is no longer capable of representing the wishes of those British people opposed to it. Therefore, by one of those paradoxes by which political truth only seems visible by being turned on its head, she supports a referendum to defend the sovereignty of the Westminster Parliament, even though a majority of the Members of the Westminster Parliament do not want such a referendum.

Not that this is a pure volte-face. There has always been a democratic tendency in Margaret Thatcher's political thought, visible in her wish that every British family should, if possible, own their own home; visible in her willingness to make a recording of the Gettysburg address; visible in her cheering on the collapse of Eastern Bloc communism slightly before it actually collapsed.

The British constitutional Monarchy is not a democratic institution. At General Elections the British people elect men and women to represent them in Parliament. Thereafter, they have never asked for any say in the way these representatives ran their affairs (though they reserve the right to grumble about the inefficiency of politicians and to rejoice in their downfall), and until the advent of Mrs Thatcher it is questionable whether they wanted such a say. The underlying principle of the British system, until twenty or so years ago, was deference. This did not necessarily mean the same thing as subservience. People were able to hold politicians in contempt while recognising that it was the function of Parliament to draw up and control the legislation which affected their lives. By the same token, people could make (usually pretty mild) jokes about the Queen or the Duke of Edinburgh without losing sight of the principle of constitutional Monarchy: which is that the Monarch has the ultimate power to ratify the legislation which Parliament decides. Of course, in the event of a Monarch choosing to block Parliamentary legislation the system would break down, but there had been no serious clash between a Prime Minister and a Sovereign for sixty or more years until the Queen's disagreement with Mrs Thatcher about South Africa.

The principle of deference is that one group of individuals literally defers to another group for political purposes. The people, having made their electoral choice, defer to Parliament's decisions. Parliament, both in the matter of law and the matter of patronage, defers to the Crown, and so does the Civil Service. The bishops, the Regius professors in the older universities, the nobility, all owe their authority to the Crown and swear allegiance to the Crown. This is not a democratic system, though when it operates well it provides checks to the possible abuse of power which might surprise a true democrat.

Margaret Thatcher's democratic revolution was only a partial success, but she did succeed in eliminating the concept of deference from many individual lives. This was most noticeably successful in her reform of Trade Union law. No system so much depends on deference and is so undemocratic (in simple terms) as the old Trades Union movement. In order to speak on behalf of its individual members a Union must make collective decisions. When this came to the exercise of a block vote at Labour Party Conferences and at its own Trades Union Congresses, it was increasingly unacceptable to its own rank and file. The idea had got abroad that democracy meant not the freedom to ask someone more engaged or better informed to make decisions on your behalf, but the freedom to make those decisions for yourself (of course, Mrs Thatcher had not invented it, she was merely one of its more colourful champions). This spelt anarchy in the Trades Unions and delivered their death blow.

How long can it be before Parliamentary democracy, based on the principle of constitutional monarchy, goes the same way as the old dinosaurs of the Labour Movement? And what will take their place? Populism is politics for the non-thinker. Fifty million people cannot all make a joint decision about the level of inflation, or the level of income tax, or about whether to go to war. These decisions have to be made for them. In the past they have been made by the Prime Minister in Cabinet, answerable on the one hand to the Sovereign and on the other to Parliament. Take away the check of Monarchy, and how long before you have removed the check of Parliament also? The British might find they have dismantled more than the Royal Household if a republican mood caught fire. But in my view there can be no doubt, if such a mood were to spread, that one of its principal authors, for all her protestations of loyalty to the Queen and to the Crown, is Margaret Thatcher.

The democratic populism on the left in Britain – represented by such figures as the former Lord Stansgate, Tony

Benn – never took hold because it sounded cranky. (This was because Benn has always appealed to logic, and human affairs are seldom run on logical lines.) Mrs Thatcher's demagogic populism made appeals to the purse and the family hearth, and to the idea that grocers' daughters and simple folk had as much right as anyone else to run the affairs of a great nation. She brought to pass what Harold Wilson, with his sauce bottles and his cheap mackintoshes, had dangled in front of the electorate as a mere dream. She would probably be horrified in one part of herself to realise the Frankenstein's monster which she has brought to birth; in another part of herself – the demagogue – she would be very far from horrified since, in the event of Britain adopting an elective Presidency, there is small doubt in anyone's mind who would consider herself most eligible for such a role. But populist whims can be difficult to extinguish. Five years ago Mr Auberon Waugh seemed a lone voice among British journalists complaining about the damage done to Britain by Mrs Thatcher and her 'New Brits'. His father, Evelyn Waugh, was asked what he would be voting in a General Election, and said that he would not presume to advise Her Majesty on the choice of Her Ministers. Things have now swung so far in an opposite direction that son Auberon can write that 'we are no longer a fit country to have a monarchy, being eaten up with rancour, hatred, aggression and envy'.* These are all good Thatcherite qualities, but if I were the Monarch, surveying the drizzly view from the windows of Buckingham Palace, I should take the words of Waugh *fils* very seriously indeed.

* *The Oldie*, December 25, 1992.

THREE

Lady Di

If the position of the Monarchy was significantly weakened by Mrs Thatcher's rise to power in 1979, she was not the only lady who was to have a profound effect – some would say a profoundly weakening effect – on the House of Windsor. It was in the first year of Mrs Thatcher's premiership that Prince Charles decided that he wanted to marry Lady Diana Spencer.

She was a nineteen-year-old infant-school teacher, living at the time in Coleherne Court in Earls Court, West London. She came from an ancient aristocratic lineage: the Spencers had received their earldom from Charles I, and they are distantly related to the poet Edmund Spenser, author of *The Faerie Queene*, a fact which caused the historian Edward Gibbon to remark: 'The nobility of the Spencers has been illustrated and enriched by the trophies of Marlborough; but I exhort them to consider *The Faerie Queene* as the most precious jewel in their coronet.'* Had he been able to see into the future, Gibbon might have revised his judgement. The eighth Earl Spencer was to father a fairy princess who far outshone *The Faerie Queene* of his poetical collateral.

Lady Diana was his third daughter. She was born on the Sandringham estate in Norfolk at her father's residence there, Park House. The story is told that when, as a young child, Lady Diana was informed that they were all driving over to nearby Sandringham to visit the Royal Family, she protested. Diana hated the 'strange' atmosphere there and kicked and screamed, and refused to go until her father told her it would be considered very bad manners if she did not join the Royal children. A strange precedent! Not much more than a dozen years later she was eagerly accepting invitations to Sandringham, and married the heir to the British Crown, His Royal Highness Charles, Prince of Wales, in St Paul's Cathedral on July 29, 1981.

Many people supposed that the marriage had been concocted by the grandmothers. The Queen Mother's friend and lady-in-waiting, Lady Fermoy, was Lady Diana's maternal grandmother, and nothing could have seemed more probable than that the old ladies had arranged the match between them. If the chronicles of Andrew Morton are to be believed, however, this would appear not to have been the case, and we learn that, before Lady Diana committed herself to Prince Charles, Lady Fermoy warned the girl strongly against marrying into the Royal Family. 'You must understand,' said Lady Fermoy, 'that their sense of humour and lifestyle are very different. I don't think it would suit you.'

* As the allusion shows, they are also related to the Dukes of Marlborough.

The differences between the Prince's famous sense of humour and that of Lady Diana did not make themselves sufficiently apparent during the summer of 1980: indeed, it was only a few days before her wedding day that Lady Diana discovered the notorious bracelet engraved with the initials 'F' and 'G' entwined – Fred and Gladys being the pet names used by His Royal Highness and his friend Mrs Parker-Bowles. While hindsight has persuaded Lady Diana that she wished at this juncture to cancel her wedding (a very usual sensation in brides two or three days before the ceremony, whether or not they discover F and G bracelets), there are those who take a different view of the Princess's approach to marriage. For such as Lady Colin Campbell, the marriage which took place in St Paul's Cathedral was the fulfilment not merely of Diana's ambitions, but of the monarchical ambitions of a whole dynasty of Spencers. Lady Colin even traces back this supposed family ambition to the lesbian love affair conducted between their ancestress Sarah, Duchess of Marlborough, with her sovereign lady Queen Anne. Not content with seducing the Queen, Duchess Sarah also bribed the Prince of Wales (later George II) with £100,000 to marry her granddaughter, Lady Diana Spencer. The bribe was not accepted, and it was not, according to Lady Colin's view of things, until 200 more years of rollicking, bodice-ripping history had passed before this voraciously ambitious family achieved their desire.* No doubt many girls who are in a position to have such dreams wonder what it would be like to marry the Prince of Wales. What makes Diana Spencer special is not merely that she achieved this aim, but that she herself turned, in consequence of her position, into a figure who eclipsed, and threatened to destroy, the Royal Family.

* Lady Colin Campbell, *Diana in Private* (1992) p.45.

*

Throughout his twenties, the Prince of Wales must have excited hopes in many young women that they might one day wear the Crown of England on their heads. Many of them, no doubt, were happy to have brief affairs with the Prince; but there must have been others who laboured under the belief that, having surrendered to him their virtue, he would surrender to them his name. The opposite was true. The very fact that they were prepared to go to bed with the Prince proved to him that they were not the virginal woman he was seeking as his bride.

We do not know how or where this obsession with virginity developed. There can be no doubt, however, that, by the time Prince Charles was thirty years old, the mood had reached fever-pitch: that he must find himself a wife, and she must be a virgin. Given the strength of his desire, the obvious place to look for such a bride was among his mother's former dominions – for example in Pakistan, where the observance of Islam (unlike the practice of Roman Catholicism, it is no barrier to marrying a British Monarch) has ensured a higher standard of sexual propriety among young females than obtained in the post-Christian Britain of the 1970s. Apart from guaranteeing for himself a wife who would observe the proprieties and know her place, the Prince could have formed an important *entente cordiale* with the Islamic world had he married a rich young Muslim. Nor, probably, would he have scorned the money and treasures brought in her dowry, which could have been greater than anything that the third daughter of a divorced English peer could possibly have secured.

It has generally been assumed – not least by those closest to the throne – since the Prince could only marry with his mother's permission, that she would choose his bride for him. It might have been better if this had been the case. (As Samuel Johnson sagely observed, 'Marriages would in general be as happy, and often more so, if they were all made by the Lord Chancellor.' How much truer for royalties than commoners.) In fact, Prince Charles did have his future bride chosen for him; but the arbiter of his destiny was neither his Sovereign nor her Lord Chancellor, but the Prince's old friend Camilla, now Mrs Parker-Bowles.

Perhaps Mrs Parker-Bowles is one of the many women in England, Wales, Scotland, Northern Ireland and the Duchy of Cornwall who believed that she might have become Queen in return for favours rendered. So indeed she might have been, if our chroniclers tell the truth, but we learn that she tired of waiting for him while he was serving in the Royal Navy, and married instead the Roman Catholic Army officer Andrew Parker-Bowles.

Though we must assume that most of what is written about the Parker-Bowleses in the newspapers is fiction, there does seem to be substantial evidence that Mrs Parker-Bowles helped the Prince choose a wife when it became apparent that this was what he needed or thought he needed. There was in reality no need for the Prince of Wales – one of nature's bachelors – to marry at all. Thanks to the fecundity of nearly all the Queen's family, there has never in recent times been a shortage of perfectly suitable heirs to the throne. A former member of his household, recalling the Prince's bachelor existence, said, 'It's very sad, really. He would never have got married, of course, because he was happy with his bachelor life. If he had his fishing tackle ready, his polo ponies saddled and a £5 note for the church collection, he was perfectly content. It was great fun. You could wake him up at six in the morning and say: "Right, Sir, we are going here"; and off we would go.' Moreover, as we are informed by one of the chroniclers, 'His friendship with Mrs Camilla Parker-Bowles, who eagerly adapted her life to his diary, dovetailed perfectly with his lifestyle.'*

Nevertheless, by the time he was thirty, people were wondering why he had not got married: the Press were wondering, politicians were murmuring about it, and his parents were worried. Any foreign Princesses deemed passable on other grounds were ruled out by the Royal Marriages Act because they were Roman Catholics. English aristocrats were unlikely to be virgins unless minors; and even a very young age was no guarantee of purity. He was on one level the most eligible bachelor in the world; but in the event, the choice of a bride seems to have been almost haphazard and clumsy, like a man who has left all his shopping for presents until Christmas Eve and dashes into the nearest department store for an armful of trinkets, however unsuitable.

It had been back in 1977 that he started to woo Lady Sarah Spencer, the eldest daughter of Lord Spencer. One of her friends at the time (presumably no longer a friend, unless Lady Sarah is very long-suffering) told Lady Colin Campbell, 'Sarah now says ... that she didn't fancy Prince Charles and that she was never interested in him as anything but a friend ... If you believe that, you'll believe anything. Of course she was interested. And she would have hung in there for as long as it took to get him, but for the fact that her emotions got the better of her. She wasn't strong-minded like Diana ... and the strain reached her. You have to understand the way the Prince treated his girl-friends to see why she wasn't up to the job – of waiting, I mean. He blew hot and cold, not only with her, but with all of them. One minute he'd be very caring, and the next it would be as if she didn't exist. After you'd seen him steadily for several days, you might not hear from him

*Andrew Morton, *Diana: Her True Story* (1993 version) p.48.

for weeks. And Sarah Spencer was not tough.'

It was on a shooting party at Althorp during his affair with Sarah Spencer that Charles had renewed his acquaint-anceship with the youngest sister, Diana, then a sixteen-year-old schoolgirl. Two years and several girlfriends later, he started to invite Diana for visits, first to Sandringham and then to Balmoral. It was at Petworth, sitting on a bale of straw, that we are told Lady Diana first really captured his heart by expressing sympathy for his demeanour at Lord Mountbatten's funeral: 'You looked so sad when you walked up the aisle at the funeral. It was the most tragic thing I've ever seen. My heart bled for you when I watched it. I thought: "It's wrong, you are lonely, you should be with somebody to look after you." ' Charles consulted with the appropriate authority, and Mrs Parker-Bowles, after a few inspections of the young woman, pronounced her mar-riageable. In October 1980 Charles and Camilla extended the honour to Lady Diana of showing her Highgrove, the house which he had lately acquired in Gloucestershire to be near the Parker-Bowleses.

Whether Lady Diana was indeed too naïve to understand the nature of the relationship between Prince Charles and Mrs Parker-Bowles – and what, indeed, the nature of that relationship has been – is not to the purpose here. Whether we believe, with Mr Morton, that she went up the aisle of St Paul's Cathedral as a lamb to the slaughter, or whether, with Lady Colin Campbell, that Lady Macbeth hardly seized a crown with more ambitious alacrity, the wedding changed everything for the House of Windsor.

On the surface of things, it would seem that the crisis in the House of Windsor was caused by the very public break-up of this marriage. In a step which was completely unprecedented, the Princess of Wales chose to make known to a journalist the details of her grievances against

Prince Charles. They were all published in a book, *Diana: Her True Story*, by Andrew Morton. This author claimed to have derived his information from the 'friends' of the Princess, but there could be no doubt that many of the most astonishing and damaging claims came direct from Lady Diana herself. 'I can *hear* my wife saying those words,' remarked Prince Charles as he read the newspaper extracts from the book.

Morton was able to reveal to the world that, a few days before the ceremony in St Paul's Cathedral, Lady Diana considered calling off the wedding when she discovered that her husband had no intention of abandoning his 'friendship' with Mrs Parker-Bowles. Sympathetic readers were able to discover that, throughout her supposedly idyllic marriage, Lady Diana had suffered from the eating disorder bulimia nervosa, that she had made suicide attempts which were in reality 'cries for help' on four or five occasions, that she persistently resented the cold and unloving attitude of her husband both towards herself and towards his two sons, and that she heartily detested his family. As soon as these disturbing details had been revealed, it was only a matter of months before the separation between the unhappy pair was announced formally from Buckingham Palace. It came at the end of an appalling year for the Queen.

The publishers of Andrew Morton's book, and in particular the Editor of the *Sunday Times*, who had paid large sums for the serial rights, were insistent that the details revealed in it would change the Monarchy forever, and possibly bring it to its knees. They and their readers were in danger of missing a point which was difficult to see because it was so obvious. Plenty of royal wives have been unhappy – Queen Alexandra's misery at the infidelities of her husband Edward VII, for example, was no secret to the world. Many women (perhaps most) have considered calling off their wedding a few days before the ceremony; and many, we are informed, overeat, vomit, hurl themselves downstairs, weep at the sight of their mothers-in-law and pour out their sorrows to unreliable 'friends'. The remarkable thing about Lady Diana Spencer is not what was revealed about her by Mr Morton; it was what she had visibly and publicly become from the very moment she walked down the aisle of St Paul's Cathedral: an object of fantasy and love for millions of people throughout the world.

The Editor of the *Sunday Times* thought that he had uncovered secret things about Lady Di which posed a great threat to Constitutional Monarchy. In fact he had only uncovered painful tittle-tattle, and the really dangerous thing about her, from the point of view of the Queen, had been staring newspaper editors in the face for more than a decade. It was not Lady Di's secret life, nor even her marriage problems, which had posed a threat to the future of the Monarchy; it was her public life, and the consequent changed attitude on the part of the Royal Family towards the Press. More than any film star in the history of Hollywood, this woman could captivate huge crowds wherever she went. She has probably been photographed more often than anyone in history, including Churchill, President Kennedy and Marilyn Monroe. And all this was apparent before her more recently developed talents as a healer and comforter of the sick – what her husband has unkindly called her 'Mother Teresa act'.

All this was new, and the Royal Family were perhaps slower than the Press to realise how damaging it was to the Crown. Before the arrival of Lady Diana Spencer as the Royal Family's star turn, the attitude of the British public to the Crown was oddly sophisticated. The huge majority of British people, as every survey has shown, wished to retain a monarchical system. They revered the Crown, and they were capable of being carried away by periods of enthusiasm for one or another member of the Royal House. But 'loving' the Queen did not mean the same as being interested by her. Continental newspapers throughout the 1950s and 1960s would carry stories about the Queen's private life and her supposedly unhappy marriage. These stories were never repeated in the English newspapers, and while that is partly because of the atmosphere of deference which unquestionably existed in those days, and which has now disappeared, it was also because, although people would have wanted to know the intimate details of the Queen's married life, they might not have wanted to read such things in a newspaper.

Editors and newspaper proprietors, even in London, were never noted for their altruism. They knew what their readers wanted. And nobody wanted the Royal Family to be like film stars, their mood swings, marital rows and favourite restaurants made into the subject of newspaper articles. People revered the Crown, but they were not really interested in the Queen, for the very simple reason that she is not really interesting.

The time for the Queen to grow worried was when the public began to respond to Lady Di in a very different manner. Her first visit to Australia, in 1982, was to set the tone for many such tours. In a country of seventeen million people, one million people were actually on the move, following the Royal couple as they journeyed from city to city. Not even the Pope was attracting crowds like this, and certainly such numbers had never massed to see the Prince of Wales in his bachelor days. Lady Di was an entirely new phenomenon in the Royal story. With the possible exception of Queen Elizabeth the Queen Mother, no member of the Royal Family had ever been so popular on a personal level.

Lady Di was loved first of all for her extraordinary photogenic beauty. Although she found the huge crowds daunting, she adapted to the role of a megastar with remarkable speed. Soon enough she was herself becoming dependent on the adulation of her fans. She was eventually to discover within herself great gifts of sympathy for those in need, for the sick and the dying; but, rather more dangerously for the family into which she had married, she had a taste for publicity. This meant that very early on she learnt that she could to a certain extent manipulate and control the Press; but only to a certain extent. If the world's newspapers and television companies made Lady Di into a star, they were to exact a price for it. The relationship between Lady Di and the Fourth Estate was comparable to the old relationship which existed between the Hanoverian Kings and the Whig Aristocracy. The one was the creature of the group; but in time each came to depend upon the other.

Up to this time, the Royal Family had viewed the Press warily and with extreme caution. Some individual members of the Royal Family, such as Prince Philip and Princess Anne, exhibited a hostility towards journalists which bordered on the paranoid. They were all, from the Queen downwards to the remotest Royal cousin, entirely unprepared for the 'new relationship' with the Press established by Prince Charles's young bride. Because of Lady Di, they all now stood in a new relationship with the Press. New rules applied, and they were not prepared for them; new newspaper proprietors such as Mr Murdoch had appeared on the scene, with none of the old attitudes of respect and decorum towards English institutions. The potential chemistry of this mixture was deadly.

Lady Diana had many qualities which remained hidden

from the world on her wedding day. From an early stage, Royal-watchers were beginning to make the comparison with another non-Royal Aristocrat, Lady Elizabeth Bowes-Lyon, who had married into the Royal Family, and made it supposedly more popular, on April 26, 1923.

Whatever one's views of either lady, both Lady Diana and the present Queen Mother are possessed of an impressive capacity to mythologise themselves and to project this personal myth* on to a credulous world. This is not to suggest that either lady is in the smallest degree either dishonest or dishonourable. But it is no inconsiderable gift to persuade the world to see oneself in one's own particular way.

From her early twenties, Lady Elizabeth Bowes-Lyon showed ambition to be the Queen of England. She was humiliated by the then Prince of Wales, and had to make do by marrying his brother, the Duke of York. She was nevertheless able to persuade herself and her children – and therefore to persuade the world – that it was the most tremendous grief to her when her 'Bertie' inherited the throne. In spite of being a very rich woman who all her life has been pampered by servants and enjoyed everything handsome about her (and nothing wrong with any of that), Queen Elizabeth has also managed to be 'the Queen Mum', supposedly never happier than when condescending to East Enders and sharing the humble plight of her loyal subjects.

Lady Diana Spencer has similar powers of self-mythology, similar abilities to make the public see her in her own terms. This is obviously not to the Royal Family's advantage. Whereas Lady Elizabeth Bowes-Lyon saw herself as the

* I do not imply, by the use of the words 'myth' or 'mythologise', to impugn the sincerity of Her Majesty or of Her Royal Highness. I am discussing the distinctive way in which they are able to share their own highly developed idea of themselves with their joyous admirers.

saviour of the Monarchy, rescuing it from the clutches
of Wallis Simpson and restoring the homely family values
which she herself exemplified, Lady Diana had a more confused self-image, which included the icon of Diana the Martyr. In this mythology of events, the carefree, innocent tom-
boy of Coleherne Court was snatched by an older and more
cynical man, who did not love her and who forced her to be
his smiling bride, however cruel and cold he was towards
her. Bravely, because this experience (added to the trauma
of her parents' divorce) had taught her to understand suffering as few people did, Lady Di was able to stretch out
healing hands to sufferers the world over. A tireless charity
worker, whether for marriage guidance or care for AIDS
victims, our Saint was there in the midst. As she said herself
to the Bishop of Norwich during her mysterious telephone
call – later unkindly ridiculed as the 'Squidgygate' tapes –
'"I understand people's suffering, people's pain, more than
you will ever know." He said, "That's obvious by what you
are doing for AIDS." I said, "It's not only AIDS, it's anyone
who suffers, I can smell them a mile away."'* Not since
Queen Anne had touched and allegedly healed the sick,
had such claims been made by a Royal personage.†

This is not to say that Lady Di has invented the qualities for
which people love her. She is quite patently and genuinely
concerned with the sick and the suffering; she is exuber-
ant, enlivened by her encounters with people, humorous

* *Sun*, August 25, 1992.
† Charles II, at his Restoration in 1660, revived the old custom of
'touching' the sick for 'the King's Evil'. The idea was that,
because anointed Kings were divinely chosen, they had special
healing powers. The practice continued throughout the reigns of
James II, William and Mary, and Anne, but was discontinued by
the Hanoverians. One of the last persons to be touched for the
evil was the scrofulous infant, Samuel Johnson.

and extraordinarily beautiful. When her admirers speak of being in love with her, this is quite seriously meant: she has attracted genuine and heart-wrenching love from her followers.

Whether the cult of Lady Di will survive the break-up of her marriage remains to be seen. The commentators have not been reticent. At the end of 1992, Paul Johnson, the wise Nestor of newspaper columnists, told readers of the *Daily Mail*: 'What the public will not tolerate is the kind of vendetta against Diana which the family pursued against the Duchess of Windsor, and for which, in Diana's case, there is no justification. If Diana is seen to be ill-treated, public sympathy will swing violently in her favour. The republicans will rejoice, the enemies of the Royal Family will rub their hands with fiendish glee, and those MPs and journalists who never miss an opportunity to undermine the institution of the Monarchy will move swiftly into action.'*

Julie Burchill, writing in the *Mail on Sunday*, took the view that it did not particularly matter any longer what the Royal Family thought of Lady Di. Burchill's message was that the Princess had, in effect, taken over already as the member of the Royalty in whom most people were interested. 'With the Windsors as they were, Britain was nothing more than a tatty tourist trap. Diana replaced its hackneyed mystique with the magic of good works and glamour. A few thousand tourists watched the Changing of the Guard at Buckingham Palace; the whole world watched the changing of Diana's clothes.'†

This, for traditionalist aristocrats like Sir Peregrine Worsthorne, was just the trouble. When Lady Diana took her two sons on a Caribbean holiday after the first Christmas of her

* December 31, 1992.

† December 13, 1992.

marital separation, Sir Peregrine allowed it to be known that 'I was by no means impressed by the many pictures of the Princess of Wales romping in the Caribbean, and if she had set out to convince me that she was a wildly unsuitable person to have custody of a boy born to be King of England, she could not have thought of a better way than to take him and his younger brother to that notorious playground of the world's rich white trash, even arranging to have the world's Press present to celebrate her deplorable taste in Christmas holiday locations.'*

Journalists are even more fickle than the public whose appetite for comment and tittle-tattle they attempt to satisfy. At the beginning of 1992 Lady Di had few critics in the Press, and by the end of it she had few friends.† That was because she had taken an enormous gamble, which the journalists called 'manipulating them'. Trapped in the misery of a marriage which had become intolerable, Lady Di would appear to have offered her husband an ultimatum. Either he let her go, or she would go in her own way. It would seem that he did not believe her, and the idea of indiscretion on this scale would not have been something which the Queen would not have believed possible until it happened. Whatever other peculiar or egotistical motives Lady Di had for revealing her unhappy story to Mr Morton, the indiscretion had its desired effect. Not surprisingly, the more stuffy commentators recalled Cosmo Gordon Lang's sermon to the exiled King after the Abdication in 1936: 'By his own will he has abdicated – he has surrendered the trust. With characteristic frankness he has told us the motive. It

Sunday Telegraph, January 10, 1993.
† For a fuller discussion, the reader is referred to Chapter Six.

was a craving for private happiness.'*

The moralisers will continue to attack her, not always aware of why there should be an alternative to their way of thinking, sometimes known in Britain as the Princess's party. The members of this group, together with their fellow-travellers and sympathisers, are not all silly men, droolingly in love with their 'Fairytale Princess'. They are people who have taken the trouble to think out the implications of what has happened in the last year, and above all to think out the implications of what has happened to the constitutional monarchy since the separation of Lady Diana from her husband.

Now that she has become a creature of the media, Lady Di's reputation will be decided by journalists. But the journalists, powerful as they might wish to be or consider themselves to be, cannot decide who is to be the future King of England. Unless the hereditary laws are radically altered,† the Crown will one day pass to Lady Diana's son William. Little as the fastidious might enjoy her tastes in friends or holiday venues, no one is going to be able to wrest her from her own children. She has shown, by her independence of spirit, that she is prepared to defy all conventions and bring a Royal Marriage to a public and painful end. One can have no doubts at all that if she is antagonised by the Royal Family in the discussions relating to the separation, she would exercise her rights to go and live abroad, taking her sons with her. That would probably spell the end of the Monarchy, or at any rate the end of the House of Windsor (which is not the same thing).‡

Throughout the summer of 1992, as the increasingly

---

* J.G. Lockhart, *Cosmo Gordon Lang* (1949) p.405.
† For some further suggestions on this, see Chapter Ten.
‡ Again, see Chapter Ten.

embarrassing stories unfolded in the newspapers, the Prince and Princess's lawyers, in close consultation with the Queen herself, played their dangerous poker game. There were threats to separate Diana from her children, which were scotched by Diana's apparent willingness to give the public details of Prince Charles's behaviour as a husband. There were petty discussions about the Princess's titles – whether or not she would be allowed to call herself Her Royal Highness. There were discussions, which were less petty, about cash, and about who should live where. All the time the Queen was trying to smooth things over and persuade the Prince and Princess of Wales to patch up their differences, for the sake of the Royal ideal and the future of the Crown. Their disastrous joint visit to Korea in the autumn was undertaken solely to fulfil an agreement with the Queen that they would have a three-month trial period of shamming. When they came home, the Prince's party lost no time in letting the world know that Diana had let down her husband by showing how miserable she was. It was at this time in London that I first began to hear the ominous calls for Lady Di's removal from the scene. Sometimes these were mock-jocular – as when the Prince's party's more puerile members called for her to be beheaded on Tower Green like the unfortunate wives of Henry VIII. Sometimes they took the form of knowing predictions – that she would 'commit suicide' by the end of 1993.

The Prince's followers seemed to have allowed a curious delusion to settle in their brains: that if the Princess could be removed from the scene, all the problems of the House of Windsor would be removed. But if this was what they thought, they were overlooking one glaringly obvious and unhappy fact: that the greatest 'problem' faced by the House of Windsor was not Lady Diana; it was her husband, His Royal Highness Prince Charles. And this would have been the case whether he had married or not.

FOUR

The Prince of
Wales

'My will henceforth is, If it ever chance that my particular interest and the general good of my Countries
should seem to go against each other, in that case,
my will is, That the latter always be preferred.' This
is a fine dialect for incipient Royalty.

Thomas Carlyle, *The Life of Frederick the Great*

Throughout November 1992, the world watched in sus-
pense to see whether the delicate GATT (General Agreement on Tariffs and Trade) negotiations would succeed,
or whether the disagreement between the United States
and France about agriculture would be irreconcilable. The
particular nub of the dispute concerned the sale of oil seed
and the respective share of the world market claimed by
French and American farmers. The more general area of
dispute concerned the Common Agricultural Policy of
the European Community. Here, not merely the United
States, but also the New Zealanders, the Canadians and the
Australians, felt that they could not be expected to open up
their markets to British and other European competitors if
the huge subsidies awarded to the French farmers by the
CAP continued to weight trade so heavily in favour of
France.

No one appeared to doubt that if the GATT talks broke

down, the world would be plunged into a trade war. The White House economic advisers suggested that the world economy would be $1,000 billion worse off if the talks collapsed. Rather than moving towards global free trade, the world would have broken down into three aggressive and highly protectionist trading zones – those dominated by Japan, the United States and Europe. The effects on the 'developing' nations would have been catastrophic. Desperate poverty, possible starvation and probable armed combat would have been the consequence of French intransigence. Since then there have been further developments, caused by the new administration in the White House, but, for the purposes of our present discussion, all that matters is to recognise the delicacy of *that particular phase* of GATT talks.

It was seen to be in everyone's interest that these talks succeeded. It was even in the French interest, as M. Jacques Delors eventually conceded after three or four weeks of international shadowboxing on the issue. It was therefore with some dismay that the world leaders read reports on December 5, 1992, of a speech delivered in French by the Prince of Wales to the Académie des Sciences Morales et Politiques in Paris.

'Because of the imperatives of trade and the unyielding rigours of "comparative advantage", do we really need to compress the traditions and vitality of rural life and culture into the straitjacket of an industry like any other?' he asked. 'One of the joys for me of being in France is that you have a particularly strong sense of those traditions – and of the ultimate cost to the human spirit of the unrelenting migration from the countryside to the big cities.'

The Prince's words were heard with especial dismay at home in Britain. Whatever his own personal views, he was surely aware of the views of the British Government and the British Foreign Office, which were fundamentally opposed to his ideas? 'I do not always do what I'm told,' he was reported as boasting to the French philosophers and academics.* The question at issue here was not whether the Prince was right or wrong about the value of rural life in France, but whether he spoke with the same voice as his mother's Government; and he clearly did not. This was not some harmless issue – such as his supposed wish that more English children studied the plays of Shakespeare or his belief that Hebridean islanders had a better 'lifestyle' than city-dwellers. It was a highly delicate political issue which his intervention could very easily have upset, for he was in danger of placing the British Government in the embarrassing position of seeming to contradict the potential Head of State. Had Charles been King when he made this speech he would actually have been the Head of State, and we should have witnessed the strange spectacle of the King taking one view of the GATT agreement and his chief Ministers taking another.

In passing, it might be worth asking what prompted Charles to make this strange outburst. One Conservative Member of Parliament said when he had read the speech, 'The Prince of Wales should be defending the people of this country, who have to pay £16 a week per family extra on average to support the French farmers and their food mountains.' What this Parliamentarian, Dr Robert Spink, perhaps did not realise was that the Prince was speaking to a very recognisable political agenda. While most of the mainstream political parties in the free world were committed to the success of GATT, there was one group, the Greens, who were committed with equal vigour to the failure of the world governments to reach economic accord.

Daily Telegraph, December 5, 1992.

The Friends of the Earth had explained ten days before the Prince's speech in Paris why they were opposed to GATT. It was because of the commitment of GATT signatories to a Multilateral Trading Organisation. In a dispute between the USA and Mexico, for instance, over 'dolphin-friendly tuna', the Organisation had ruled that individual countries did not have the right to apply 'extraterritorial environmental measures' to their problems. In the Prince's words, 'do we really need to compress the traditions and vitality of rural life into the straitjacket of an industry like any other?'

The question which arises here is not whether the Prince happens to be right or wrong over the matter of French agriculture. Nor is it entirely a question – though this is a very important matter – of whether he directly contradicts Her Majesty's Government in areas which could affect the peace and stability of mankind. It is also the question of whom he speaks *for*. Perhaps he thinks that he speaks for himself, though there is abundant evidence that all the famous speeches which he has delivered to the world – about architecture, the environment or cheese – have been written for him by someone else. In the case of the GATT speech to the Académie, he was being used as a pawn by a powerful international pressure group. At a time when the French were feeling particularly belligerent towards Britain and when the French farmers especially were ready for a trade war, it was in the interest of such pressure groups to wish to embarrass the British. A British Prime Minister was on the point of hosting the meeting of the European leaders in Edinburgh. The Greens and the pressure group Friends of the Earth were committed to crippling the GATT talks. Prince Charles's speech in Paris in fact failed to wreck GATT, but it had a better chance than most such utterances. To some observers, the speech may have displayed his famous intellectual daring and independence.

To others he seemed simply like a ventriloquist's dummy mouthing the ideas of cranky pressure groups.

Prince Charles is not notably cleverer than his mother, grandfather or great-grandfather, but he entirely lacks their intellectual humility. At his father's disastrous insistence, Prince Charles was not given a conventional education; he was sent to Gordonstoun, not a noted centre of intellectual excellence. The combination of bullying and toadyism which he encountered at this German educational establishment set in the rigours of the Scottish Highlands will hardly have given him an accurate idea of his own capabilities, and indeed he left the school and went up to Cambridge with a wholly inflated sense of his own cleverness. Had he been sent to a school such as Eton where there are some genuinely clever boys and masters, he might have come to understand his actual level. He is not, as his sycophantic followers have been assuring him for twenty years, 'an intellectual'. Unlike first-rate minds he does not always understand what he is saying. For example, inspired by his mentor Sir Laurens van der Post, the Prince decided that the 'simple life' is preferable to the unspiritual existence pursued by most city-dwellers in the West. This inspired the Prince, most unwisely, to make a television documentary film about the Hebridean island of Berneray.

At the sight of the Prince arriving on this island by aeroplane and car, and having an abundance of extremely expensive luggage carried for him by underlings, it was hard to restrain a smile – particularly when he began to lecture the local inhabitants about the beauty of the simple life. Accompanied by one of the best-paid British television 'personalities', Miss Selina Scott, Prince Charles visited a turf-roofed hovel which had been deserted by its miserable inhabitants; the Prince said how sad he found it that people no longer lived in such dwellings. Miss Scott enthusiastically agreed. On this particular island, there are gale-force winds for much of the year. During the week of the Prince's visit we saw that it was with the greatest difficulty that the children were able to open the door of the school, such was the force of the wind. Quite understandably, their parents wished to live in windproof bungalows with metal-framed draught-excluding windows with double glazing. The Prince wished they could see that the old turf-roofed hovels were much more in tune with the environment.

Having delivered himself of this view, the Prince flew home to Highgrove, the substantial country house which he bought for himself in Gloucestershire from his income as Duke of Cornwall.* The Duchy comprises 126,000 acres of property in twenty counties, though most of its real estate is to be found between the Isles of Scilly and Dorset. There is probably no reason to suppose that Prince Charles is a better or worse landlord than the other great property-holders in Britain, such as the Oxford and Cambridge Colleges or the Duke of Westminster. His critics would point to the fact that he did nothing to save the Cornish tin mines which had been in operation since Roman times, and that he had been a hard taskmaster to the tenants. In 1984, the Prince was persuaded to have a change of investment policy. Assets were sold off, and the policies of agricultural expansion and 'conservationism' were sacrificed to considerations of the highest possible investment income. Three years later, the Secretary of the Duchy was able to say, 'The Duchy is stronger today than twenty years ago. Its investment is better spread.' Cynics noted that this had been achieved by exorbitant rent rises for the Duke of Cornwall's tenants and

*His income from the Duchy of Cornwall makes him the fourteenth richest man in Great Britain. See Anthony Holden, *Charles* (1988) pp.42 ff.

the closing down of such pet schemes as the 'model farms', which, one might have thought, would have appealed to the Prince's traditionalist approach to the countryside.

No reasonable person would object to a landlord wishing to get as much out of his property as possible and to manage his investments wisely. They might only begin to feel dissatisfaction at being lectured by such a landlord on the beauties of old-fashioned agriculture and the simple life. Likewise, only the strictest puritan would expect the Prince of Wales or any other Royal personage to have a blameless sexual career. It was his persistent sermonising, the explicit claim that his views of life – on farming, on architecture, on the environment – would bring people not merely closer to peace but closer to God which made malicious ears so willing to listen to the so-called 'Camillagate' tapes, transcripts alleged to be of recorded telephone conversations between the Prince and his friend Mrs Parker-Bowles.

Charles:	One has to feel one's way along, if you know what I mean.
Camilla:	Mm. You're awfully good at feeling your way along.
Charles:	Oh, stop! I want to feel my way along you, all over you and up and down you and in and out . . .
Camilla:	Oh.
Charles:	Particularly in and out . . .
Camilla:	Oh . . .
Charles:	The trouble is, I need you several times a week.
Camilla:	Mm. So do I. I need you all the week. All the time.
Charles:	Oh, God. I'll just live inside your trousers or something. It would be much easier.

Camilla:	(Laughs) What are you going to turn into, a pair of knickers? (Both laugh) Oh, you're going to come back as a pair of knickers.
Charles:	Or, God forbid, a Tampax! Just my luck!*

It is cruel to quote these words. On the other hand, it would not be entirely fair to omit them either. They have become part of the story, whether any of us likes it or not, and if one were to consider the recent history of the Royal Family without alluding to the notorious tapes (however they were obtained, by whom they were obtained, and for what purpose – that is all another story) it would be exhibitionistic to leave them out, just as it is distasteful to remember them. After forty years of earnestly trying to do his best, and after ten or fifteen years of very public service in which the Prince has offered us his opinions on everything from gardening to global warming, from Shakespeare to Jung, from the language of architecture to the future of the Third World, it must be dismaying for him to realise that the public at large can probably only remember two of his utterances: his comparison of a proposed scheme to modernise the National Gallery to a 'monstrous carbuncle'; and his wish to be reincarnated as Mrs Parker-Bowles's Tampax.

The British royalist who contemplates the career of the Prince of Wales must sing the National Anthem with a particular fervour: – 'Long to reign over us – God save the Queen!' Not only would the Prince of Wales's marital status make it difficult for him to become the Supreme Governor of the Church, it would also make a nonsense of the Windsor

New Idea, January 23, 1993 pp.22–23.

tradition that the King should have an exemplary domestic life. Though wisdom might be granted him with age, it has to be said that many of his public utterances to date have come perilously close to being 'unconstitutional'; and, far from appearing to mind all this, the Prince positively relishes it.

If we were concerned in this book in passing judgement on the personages of the Royal Family, it would be necessary to say in the Prince's defence that he has had a life which would have taxed many others in his position. On the one hand he has been trained (with considerable lack of wisdom) by his parents for the position of being King. On the other hand, since his mother was a very young woman when he was born, it was obvious from the first that no one wished Prince Charles to inherit the throne – or, at least, not until he was advanced in years. Since the Queen was generally acknowledged to be an exemplary monarch, no one could wish Prince Charles to be King without wishing dead his highly esteemed and wholly admirable mother.

Charles's training was all, therefore, of a contingent character. His life has been one large 'AS IF!' He was never allowed, as most young people might be, to find his *métier* and then pursue it, for the *métier*, if he found it, would have involved the death of the one person supremely capable of keeping the British Monarchy flourishing in the mid-twentieth century. Thus it was, from the moment he was sent to his appalling boarding school to the blunder about the GATT talks in December 1992, that Prince Charles has been a tinkerer, a potterer, a dabbler with this and that. After school, a visit to Timbertop, the Bushland annexe of Geelong Grammar School, Australia. Presumably, the bright idea behind this experience (Prince Charles was said to hate it) was that he should acquaint himself with the Commonwealth of which he might one day be Head.

Then, since he was the Prince of Wales, he was sent to the University of Aberystwyth for a few weeks to acquire a smattering of Welsh in a language laboratory. Then off to Cambridge, where he changed course several times. Then a spell in the Army. Then a spell in the Navy. And after that – there has been no fixed career, no obvious role for him to follow.

Of course, there is no reason why Princes should have 'jobs'. Had he not been brought up from an early age to believe that he was being trained to be King, Charles might have been perfectly happy tending his country house, Highgrove, where he is said to be a keen gardener, playing polo, hunting, and mixing with his loyal circle of slightly eccentric friends. But how would anyone feel if they were trained for a specific role, only to be told, when that 'training' was nearly done, that they could not start the job until they were seventy years of age? Would not a young doctor emerging from medical school feel some sense of frustration if he or she were told they could not practise until they were old; and a lawyer who could not be called to the Bar until they were past the age when most people retire? The then Prince of Wales (Bertie), during the celebratory service at St George's Chapel, Windsor, for the Diamond Jubilee of Queen Victoria, remarked in an audible voice to an equerry, 'I have no objection to praying to the Eternal Father, but I have heard enough about the Eternal Mother.'

It would seem very likely that Prince Charles's irresponsible old great-uncle, Lord Mountbatten, had led the boy to understand that 'Lilibet' would stand down as soon as her son was ready to take over the reins of office. Nothing could have been further from the Queen's mind, and, as her son's unfortunate life unfolded, she was hardened in her resolve not to abdicate. In her Christmas Broadcast in 1991, she

even took the unprecedented step of reminding listeners
and viewers all over the world that she was ever-mindful
of her Coronation oath to be Queen *for life*. Prince Charles
was furious, and the coldness led to a period when mother
and son were not on speaking terms.

He is in fact one of the very few people in the world
who has never had to 'prove himself', and yet, perhaps for
that very reason, his life has been one long attempt at self-
justification. All the public speechifying, all the patronage
of worthy charities, his concern for British cities – both their
architectural heritage and the lives of the urban poor – have
an air of strain about them. It is as though, like a constipated
man at his stool, he is struggling and forcing himself to bring
to pass what, in happier circumstances, might be expected
to follow quite naturally. During a coast-to-coast tour of the
United States in 1977, an arduous itinerary of public speaking engagements, visits, banquets, receptions, an American
journalist remarked, 'My God! That guy works so hard you'd
think he was running for office!' His biographer, Anthony
Holden, quoting this remark, added, 'In a way, he is.'*

But of course he isn't running for office, he is merely
marking time, and since that remark was made and Mr
Holden's first book about the Prince was published we
have seen the sad effects of the Prince's boredom and
self-doubt.

In Mr Holden's second biography of Prince Charles, published nine years later, we read of a fascinating encounter
between Margaret Thatcher and the Prince of Wales, which
took place at Kensington Palace on March 25, 1988.

There had been considerable feelings of dismay from
the Conservative wing of the House of Commons about
Charles's intervention in political questions – such as his

*Anthony Holden, *Charles, Prince of Wales* (1979) p.272.

concern for the unemployed and the plight of the homeless in inner cities. Mr Norman Tebbit (now Lord Tebbit) had said on television, 'I suppose the Prince of Wales feels extra sympathy towards those who've got no job because in a way he's got no job, and he's prohibited from having a job until he inherits the throne . . . He's forty, yet he's not been able to take responsibility for anything, and I think that's really his problem.' Another Conservative MP, Tony Marlow, had decided, on the strength of Charles's moderately expressed concern for those less well-off than himself, that he was a dangerous pinko, 'unfit to be king'. Since Mrs Thatcher had reformed the Trades Unions, the Health Service and the Nationalised Industries, why should she not – asked her right-wing 'radical' followers – set about reforming the Monarchy?

On that sad morning, Lady Day, 1988, it was the Prime Minister who, in physical terms, called on the Prince; but in actual terms, it was he who came to her, 'cap in hand'. He had arranged the meeting in the hope that he could work himself back into the Government's favour, and even get some concessions from the Prime Minister which had been hitherto denied him by his mother: a few pathetic little things to do. Would it be possible, he asked the Prime Minister, for him to preside over the State Opening of Parliament in his mother's absence? The Prime Ministerial answer to this question was a modified Yes, but if he did so it would only be as a 'Lord Commissioner', and he would only be allowed to read the Queen's Speech (written of course by the Prime Minister) from a bench in the Chamber rather than from the Throne.

Then Charles raised the delicate question of whether he might assume some title which gave him a greater significance in the running of State affairs. Might he not be declared Prince Regent? The making of this request is one of the odder things done by Prince Charles; a Regent, after all, is only necessary if the Monarch has ceased to be able to perform her functions, and Queen Elizabeth II was still very much in control of things when this request was made. So, unsurprisingly, the Prime Minister turned him down.

There was, however, one task for which she considered him to be eligible: the Governorship of Hong Kong. In the event, this task was seen to be too delicate for someone as insensitive as the Prince. After the Tianamen Square massacre in Peking in 1989, the Governorship of Hong Kong and the task of handing over the colony to the Chinese when the British Lease expires in 1997 were given to a professional politician. For a sad interlude, however, Charles had been under the impression that he was going to have what he had for so long coveted: a real job, a position in the world.*

In the aftermath of the Prince's separation from his wife, it was inevitable that outside observers should 'take sides'. Those who felt that his wife had treated him shabbily by making public so many of her private marital discontents were perhaps tempted to overemphasise Charles's many good qualities – his famous sense of humour, his fondness for the old 1950s radio *Goon Show*, his wish to do well by 'his people', his harmless pursuits such as foxhunting and painting in watercolours. It was emphasised, and this could hardly be denied, that he was one of the best-dressed men in the Western world. All these undoubted merits would need to be placed in the balance if we were conducting a judgement of Prince Charles's character, but we are not.

Our subject is the Royal crisis – whether there is one, whether there would be one if the Queen were to die. And

*Anthony Holden, *Charles: a Biography* (1988) pp.212 ff.

from that point of view, one has to say that Prince Charles does not merely contribute to the difficulties of the Royal House, he is the difficulty. The rest – the fact that some parts of the population wish the Queen were not so rich, or that the Patronage system should be reformed or abolished, or that certain newspapers have published certain photographs of the Duchess of York, or that an American biographer may be unkind enough to spill the beans about the Duke of Edinburgh's alleged indiscretions – all this is in a sense irrelevant to the central concern. That concern can be summarised in one sentence: can the British Monarchy survive? And the only thing which could seriously make it difficult for it to survive is the survival of Prince Charles.

There are quite simple reasons for this. The House of Windsor, under the tutelage of George V, George VI and Elizabeth II, has evolved a very distinct and a very workable role for the Monarchy. It is a symbol of family values; it is religious; it is constitutional. Because of the way that Charles has led his life, he is now woefully unsuited to fulfil any of these three functions. He has separated from his wife, and so can hardly provide the sort of icon of virtuous domesticity which was given to the world by his parents. He inherits peculiar difficulties in the religious field,* but he has compounded these difficulties by allowing his marriage to collapse. It was over the question of divorce that Edward VIII was sent into exile, and (less importantly) it was because she was 'mindful of the Church's teachings' that Princess Margaret, the Prince's aunt, was unable to follow her own inclinations and marry Group Captain Townsend, whom she loved. Moreover, as I have shown, Prince Charles has made life very difficult for himself by consistently speaking out on delicate public issues, to the point where Ministers

*See Chapter Eight.

of the Crown can make very slightly threatening jokes about his being unemployed.

Given the way in which Charles has lived in the last forty years, it would be necessary, were he to inherit his mother's throne tomorrow, to revise the traditional relationship between Church and State, to amend the Coronation Oath and to think very seriously about the Monarch's constitutional role; for if the Prince's intervention in the GATT dispute were a harbinger of things to come, no British Prime Minister could risk having him as King without curbing his constitutional role almost to the point where he was purely decorative.

This is the reality of the thing, and it is the reason that Charles himself will almost certainly be persuaded to stand down in favour of his son William and to renounce any claim which he might still have to the throne. If he could not be persuaded to do this, however, the British people would simply have to live with the fact. That it would provoke a crisis, there cannot be any doubt. But the Monarchy has survived crises before, and there is no particular reason for supposing that it could not survive crises again. It is not as though Prince Charles were entirely devoid of king-like qualities.

Indeed, it could be said, without straining after paradox, that the crucial flaw in the House of Windsor was their desire to be good monarchs. The strength of a constitutional Monarchy such as has evolved in Britain over the last two centuries is that the system works perfectly well, whether the Monarch is 'good' or 'bad' at their task. By most of the hard-working standards established by the House of Windsor, Queen Victoria could be seen as deplorably 'bad' at her job. 'Anything to please' – Edward VIII's highly ironic and oft-repeated little catch-phrase – had never been Victoria's rule of life. Unlike Queen Elizabeth II or Prince Charles, she seldom undertook public duties, she made no attempt to disguise her feelings about individual politicians, she was unashamedly partisan in constitutional questions and idle in her discharge of the minimal duties required of her. (She even refused, for many years of her widowhood, to take part in the State Opening of Parliament ceremonies.) Yet it could be argued that there was never a period when the British Monarchy was stronger than in Queen Victoria's reign.

True, Prince Charles's faults are very different from Queen Victoria's. She was indolent, where he is 'workaholic'. She was unabashed by personal unpopularity; he is neurotically hypersensitive about his reputation in the Press. But the history of Victoria's reign triumphantly demonstrates that a successful constitutional Monarchy can be maintained for decades without a markedly competent Monarch at the head of it. No one can predict how long Queen Elizabeth II will live, but there is every possibility that Charles's reign, if it happened at all, would be of extremely short duration. If the future of the Monarchy depended upon him alone, it would be sad indeed. But the office is larger than the individuals who succeed to it. He would no doubt try to be a conscientious and dutiful King. There is a great poignancy in the fact that the elaborate 'training' he has received for this office is precisely what makes him such an unsuitable candidate for it. But, if he were to succeed to the throne, the public could wait for better days; and in the short duration of his reign – who knows? – they might in some small areas be pleasantly surprised.

Things would never be the same, however, as in the palmier days of his mother's reign. Even supporters of the Prince would feel that there were only very limited areas where he could be expected to shine. They would hope that he would fulfil his constitutional functions, but they would fear, every time that he made a public speech, that he would say either something tactless or something foolish. They would have to play down his religious role, and, when he stood on the balcony of Buckingham Palace, he would either be there alone or in the forlorn company of his two sons. As the Victorian critic who had seen a production of *Antony and Cleopatra* remarked, 'How unlike the home life of our own dear Queen.'

FIVE

The Queen

When I broke the news to Margaret and Lilibet
that they were going to live in Buckingham Palace,
they looked at me in horror. 'What!' Lilibet said. 'You
mean forever?'

Marion Crawford, *The Little Princesses*

When the Queen was in her early teens, it was decided
that she should be instructed in the mysteries of the British
Constitution, and she was sent off to Sir Henry Marten,
the Vice-Provost of Eton College, just down the road from
Windsor Castle. Sometimes Princess Elizabeth attended
upon Sir Henry in his study – he had an endearing habit of
chewing on sugar lumps as he expounded the thoughts of
Walter Bagehot, the Victorian editor of the *Economist*, whose
views on constitutional matters are seldom questioned by
any modern advisers to the Royal Family.

Bagehot wrote at a time when franchise was being extended to all males, for the first time in British history. The
Reform Act of 1867 allowed a parliamentary vote to the
unskilled labouring class. 'What I fear', Bagehot wrote in
the Preface to the second edition of *The English Constitution*,
'is that both our political parties will bid for the support of
the working man: that both of them will promise to do as he

likes if he will only tell them what it is.' Bagehot, in other words, saw democracy, in the popular sense of the word, rearing its Gorgon head, and he feared the consequences. In these circumstances, he saw the Monarchy as an institution of crucial importance. Monarchy, in his view, is strong government because it is 'intelligible'. Unlike the democrats of fourth-century BC Athens, the Victorian English did not have a slave class. 'But we have whole classes unable to comprehend the idea of a constitution – unable to feel the least attachment to impersonal laws. Most indeed do vaguely know that there are other institutions besides the Queen and some rules by which she governs. But a vast number like their minds to dwell more upon her than upon anything else, and therefore she is inestimable.'

Bagehot appears to be reducing the Monarchy to the role of a sideshow, useful for distracting the ignorant multitudes while the actual business of government continues, as it has done before, in the hands of the statesmen. But, within the Parliamentary system, he believed that the Sovereign did have some function – as an emblem of family life, as a religious figurehead, as the 'head of society', as a moral example; and, in her dealings with ministers, as an adviser. Successive generations of modern Prime Ministers have piously repeated Bagehot's view that the function of a constitutional Monarch was to warn, to encourage and to advise.

When one examines Bagehot's 'sketch', as he calls it, of the constitution, and compares it with the original from which he was taking a likeness, one is arrested by the distortion of his view. 'We shall find', he wrote, 'that it is only during the present reign that in England the duties of a constitutional sovereign have ever been well performed.' One would not have expected a Victorian journalist of Bagehot's standing to have been positively insulting about Queen Victoria, but the compliment here is distinctly double-edged. Bagehot knew perfectly well that Queen Victoria's relations with her ministers were initially stormy, but ultimately docile and acquiescent. After *The English Constitution* was published, as the Queen sank further and further into introspection and depression, she all but abandoned the responsibilities of office for decades, though losing no opportunity to interfere with matters of foreign policy when they affected either her far-flung family or her whim. If Bagehot wished to claim that Queen Victoria was the great example of how to perform the roles of a constitutional Monarch, he might have been taking the same view of the sovereign as W. S. Gilbert took of the House of Lords, which 'did nothing in particular, and did it very well'.

The person who could, however, be said to be a Monarch cast in Bagehot's mould, and who has followed his injunctions most slavishly, is Elizabeth II. She has been a Monarch who was always prepared to seem useless and busy at the same time. For, if Bagehot is her guide, her parents are her role model.

George VI and Queen Elizabeth (now the Queen Mother) occupied the monarchical role at a peculiar period in British history. While 'Lilibet' sat with Sir Henry Marten, hearing him crunch sugar lumps and expound the works of Bagehot, the King and Queen were playing a crucial part in Churchill's war leadership. Sir Winston Churchill had been a leading light in the 'King's Party' – the small group of people who believed that King Edward VIII should not be forced to abdicate in 1936. As such, Churchill was viewed with deep suspicion by the Royal Family, and by Queen Elizabeth in particular. When Churchill became the wartime Prime Minister in 1940, however, Queen Elizabeth was prepared to put her hostility to Wallis Simpson beneath her duties as Queen-consort. It did not take long for feelings of close friendship to develop between Churchill and the new King.

Nearly all British people who lived through the Second World War felt that the King and Queen did immeasurable good. The King wore uniform throughout the war. Even when Buckingham Palace was bombed, the King and Queen refused to leave London, though this meant that (like many poor London families) they had to be separated from their children. (For their safety, the Princesses Elizabeth and Margaret Rose were immured in Windsor Castle.) Queen Elizabeth's famous comment after the bombing of Buckingham Palace – 'Now we can look the East End in the face' – was rightly seen as characteristic of her, and the King's, plucky approach.

The Second World War was, in fact, a godsend to the British Royal House. Only three years before the outbreak of the war, the Abdication crisis looked as if it might bring the Monarchy to an end. The war made the British feel that they needed the Monarchy, and the King and Queen could not have presented a better image of themselves during the years of hostility. They used ration books. They visited hospitals and battlefields and bomb-sites. They gave meaning to the cliché that the Monarchy could provide a 'focus of national unity' during a time of crisis. 'This war', wrote Churchill to the King, 'has drawn the Throne and the people more closely together than was ever before recorded, and Your Majesties are more beloved by all classes and conditions than any of the princes in the past.' This sounds like pure flattery, but it was simply true.

Urged on by her parents' example, Queen Elizabeth II, when she inherited the throne, continued to visit her people as often as her parents had done during the war. In wartime there was some obvious value in the King appearing in urban areas devastated by bombs. The habit survived into peacetime. Hospitals, factories, old people's homes, shopping malls, motorways, railway stations – it did not seem possible for any of these places to be rebuilt or to extend themselves without receiving a Royal visit. Ever anxious to oblige, the new Queen visited them all, as well as keeping up a taxing programme of world travel and being far more conscientious than Queen Victoria would ever have been about the political aspect of her functions: the signing of papers, the consulting with Prime Ministers, and so forth. Because the Queen did all these things with such alacrity and such professionalism, and such lack of fuss, it was assumed that this was a necessary part of her job; and when her children were old enough they were taught to do the same. Many of her subjects could be forgiven for believing that it was the Queen's 'job' to travel constantly, unveiling plaques, making visits and shaking hands with lord mayors. None of these journeys was necessary, and it is certain that none of them was constitutionally necessary. But they have been highly characteristic of the reign, and it would probably be difficult now for them to stop altogether.

Given the tireless service which the Queen has given to her country, the attitude of the British Press to her famous year of misfortunes in 1992 was, to say the least, surprising.

When the fire broke out in Windsor Castle on November 20, 1992, there were unforgettable sights of the Queen, pacing about among the firemen and helpers in her wellington boots and her headscarf, visibly distressed and yet trying to offer what help she could. It was her forty-fifth wedding anniversary, and her husband was abroad. She was at Windsor again the next day, still in the headscarf and wellingtons. Although she is a woman in her mid-sixties, she seemed like a resourceful but unhappy child, a Christopher Robin-like figure.

It must have been with some astonishment that many British people opened their newspapers that morning and discovered that the more oafish elements of the Press were choosing to continue their onslaught on the House of Windsor. If ever there was a morning to 'lay off' the Queen, this was surely it. And yet on they went, asking who was going to pay for the repair of the castle, estimated at £60 million. The Queen, of course, had had no chance to say anything about the matter, and nobody knew whether she intended to make a contribution to the restoration of Windsor. It was just assumed that she would not. The arguments about whether the taxpayer or the Sovereign should bear the cost of official residences were perfectly legitimate. The fact that the newspapers were choosing to have such arguments on such a day, however, looked like sadism. When, the following day, nursing a heavy cold, the Queen went to the Mansion House and made her by now famous speech about 1992 having been an *annus horribilis*, she had become an object of pity, at least in some circles. Even this was something which could be held to her charge. When the Monarch has become an object of pity, said Sir Peregrine Worsthorne, it is time for loyal monarchists to declare for a republic.

Certainly, the unsympathetic – some would say ungallant – newspaper coverage of the Queen and the Windsor fire was very surprising. I at least believed that most people in England had some respect for the Queen and – though it sounds absurdly sentimental to say so – some love. Could I have been wrong? What had this woman ever done to make her an object of such cruelty? From childhood, she had been thrust into the role of a public servant. She had helped her father George VI with running what he called 'The Firm' until his early death, when she was only twenty-five. Since then, she has been a full-time Head of State. Unlike Queen

Victoria, Elizabeth II has been excessively conscientious in the fulfilment of all her duties. No President in the world has ever held office for so long, or worked so hard or served their country so faithfully. How could it be, on the simple level of natural gratitude, that the British could not have contrived to be a little kinder to the Queen in her hour of sadness?

Having reflected on the matter, I think I have come up with some possibly plausible answers. Perhaps – who knows? – they throw some light on the part the Queen has played in the decline of the House of Windsor. For it is customary to say that 'for forty years the Queen has not put a foot wrong'. If that were true, there would be no crisis. But a crisis there certainly is, and the Queen must have played some part in causing it, though I suspect that her fault might, paradoxically, be in her near-faultlessness. The British have very understandably come to take her for granted; and, in a mood which is not justifiable, but understandable, they have come to feel that she is such a hard act to follow that maybe the act itself should be wound up. Is that a possible view of events?

It is very difficult to classify the Queen or to write about her intelligently. Most historians of the Royal Family or experts on such matters can only fall back on the language of worship and sycophancy when they attempt to do so; and, understandably, that provokes those who find it nauseating into wholly unfair assaults on the Queen herself. One possible reason for the Royal Family's current 'image problems' with the media is that, although the Queen has been admired and loved, I think it would be a mistake to suppose that the British Royal Family had ever, strictly speaking, been popular. At the time when it was arguably strongest, during the reign of Queen Victoria, the Monarch was actively hated by the majority of her subjects.

Certainly, no one has ever admired Queen Elizabeth II because they thought she was interesting in herself. Virtuous, bright-eyed, surprisingly good-looking when met 'in the flesh'; all these things might be said about the Queen, but she has not been revered so much for her personal qualities as for what she represented and what she was. At the time of her Coronation, a reverence was felt for her office which was quasi-religious, which would account for the extraordinary hostility meted out to any who ventured to criticise her in any degree. In 1956, Malcolm Muggeridge, writing in the *New Statesman*, had coined the phrase 'the Royal soap opera' and pointed out that while the Queen was popular with her lower-class subjects she was held in some derision by those better born. 'It is duchesses, not shop assistants, who found the Queen dowdy, frumpish and banal,' he wrote. The article was syndicated and sold to the United States, and was republished to coincide with a Royal visit to America in 1957. Reprinted with the headline 'Does England Really Need a Queen?', the article caused enormous offence. Muggeridge himself was accused of calling the Queen 'dowdy, frumpish and banal'. British Empire Loyalists posted excrement through Muggeridge's door, daubed his house with paint and wrote to express their pleasure that his teenage son had been killed in a skiing accident. ('One Muggeridge the less!') Lord Altrincham, at about the same time, writing in the *National and English Review*, expressed comparably moderate reservations about the Monarchy. He ventured to say that, in the Queen's speeches, 'the personality conveyed by her utterances which are put into her mouth is that of a priggish schoolgirl, captain of the hockey team, a prefect and a recent candidate for confirmation'. Lord Strathmore, the Queen's cousin, said that if he had a gun, he would have shot Lord Altrincham for writing these words; and some loyal member of the public struck Altrincham in the face.

But just because Altrincham and Muggeridge excited public outrage, it would be wrong to suppose that the public attitude towards the Royal Family was one of slavish interest. True, there were those who collected mugs or biscuit tins emblazoned with the faces of Prince Philip, Queen Elizabeth II and their relations. But nearly all royal jokes of the last forty years – on television, stage, or radio – have been gentle meditations on the Queen's essential dullness. The supposedly 'satirical' mood of the 1960s produced jokes about the essentially bourgeois qualities of the Queen and her family, the fact that they were unfashionably dressed, dowdy and intellectually limited. When she visited the Emperor Hirohito of Japan, she had an hour or so of private conversation with the divinely born potentate. When she emerged, she is supposed to have remarked, 'That man can talk of nothing except tropical fish'; he, for his part, was remarking testily to his entourage, 'That woman can talk of nothing except horses.' It is on this scarcely exciting level that the Queen was perceived. 'Loving' the Queen did not mean, for her average subject, being interested by her.

Throughout the 1950s and 1960s, the British public would be periodically amused by rumours that some continental newspaper, usually an Italian one, was running the story of some royal 'scandal' – usually the marital difficulties of the Queen or her sister, or both. British newspapers, partly for reasons of politeness and deference to the Crown, never published such stories. But editors and newspaper proprietors, even in London, were never as high-minded as all that. They knew what their readers wanted. And nobody wanted the Royal Family to be like film stars, their mood-swings, marital rows and favourite restaurants made into the subject of newspaper articles. People revered the Crown, but they were not really interested in the Queen for the very simple reason that she is not really interesting. Her uninterestingness is a positive asset.

Her husband and her son had both, in their slightly poignant ways, attempted to capture the public interest as figures 'in their own right'. Prince Philip did this by occasional ill-judged speeches on the nature of British industry, expressing the wish that workers and management would 'pull their finger out'. Even before his famous outbursts about modern architecture or the environment, Prince Charles let it be known that he held a number of deeply sincere 'views' on issues of the day. We have already discussed the political implications of some of Prince Charles's public outbursts, but in general what these speeches by Prince Charles and his father revealed was what we had all suspected before they made them: that there was nothing interesting about Royal personages at all. Indeed, there was always something extremely embarrassing about men of clear intellectual limitations attempting to form sentences which would impress the average newspaper reader. In a world of real industrialists, real intellectuals, real naturalists, they could not compete. When they opened their mouths, it was time to shuffle and look hard at one's feet.

While it probably did not do to say this too loudly, and while it might have grieved the Queen when she realised that this was what people thought of her and her family, it was not necessarily a drawback. If the Royal Family had been cleverer or more interesting, people might have been tempted to suppose that they were there because of their own merit, rather than simply because they were royal; and as soon as anyone supposed that the Monarch deserved to be the Monarch, that would be the end of the Monarchy. One would have replaced the whole concept of hereditary monarchy for an elective meritocracy.

Having been drilled in the Bagehot mould, the Queen has faithfully made herself into the Monarch of that constitutionalist's famous essay. But was Bagehot right? And, even if he was right in the 1860s and 1870s, do his words still make sense when applied to the Britain of the mid-1990s?

Bagehot, who viewed with such misgivings the extension of political suffrage to the labouring classes, would hardly have felt at home in the age of television and popular culture – a world to which, willy-nilly, the Queen belongs. He would have been unable to conceive (as would anyone in the pre-cinematic age) the importance of visual – filmed or televised – images for the mass culture. At the opening of his discussion of the Monarchy he wrote, 'Most people when they read that the Queen walked on the slopes at Windsor – that the Prince of Wales went to the Derby – have imagined that too much thought and prominence were given to little things. But they have been in error . . .' To read a newspaper report in Victorian England which described the Queen walking in her garden or her son at the races might, indeed, have run the danger of making too much of 'little things'. In the age of mass culture, the little things are in danger of seeming as if they are the only things. The Queen has always been willing to use the popular media. With the marriage of her son, however, the Royal House became, as we have seen, something different: almost an extension of Hollywood, with many of the inevitable attendant calamities.

So Bagehot's praise for the 'little things' would probably now have to be modified. If the medium of television has emphasised the 'little thing' above the great and unseen virtues of the monarchical system, then might not that system itself have been trivialised out of existence?

Bagehot also seems questionable in his assumption that a Monarch's only function in a modern political context is to warn, encourage or advise. Just as he wrote before the age of mass culture, he wrote before the political exploitation of mass culture and those great political movements which were only made possible because of radio and newsreel: Stalinism and Nazism. The political dangers which face even so conservative (with a small 'c') a country as Britain in the twentieth century would have been quite inconceivable to anyone living in the nineteenth century. True, Bagehot contemplates the tempestuous European events of 1848, just as he was to contemplate the turbulent history of France in and around 1870, and he found that he preferred the House of Lords and the House of Commons. But no nineteenth-century demagogue had the resources which were to be placed at the disposal of twentieth-century demagogues: the microphones, the film camera and the weapons of destruction.

Even if one does not fear the ultimate calamity in Britain, the arrival of some fascist or Stalinist dictator – and it seems, on the face of things, a rather unlikely eventuality – one is compelled to recognise that our world is a much nastier world than Bagehot's, and one in which politicians have far more opportunities of wrecking societies and individual lives through the abuse of power. In such a world as this, one has to notice, observing the political scene in Europe over the last half-century or so, that it is in apparently free and apparently elective systems that the worst abuses of power have taken place. Once elected, the despot receives no check on his or her power. It is in such a dangerous world as ours that one begins to see the virtues of the British monarchical system, where the Head of State (there through no merit of her own, solely through birth) has the right and duty to check the abuse of Parliamentary power; and where the Cabinet and Parliament exercise a perpetual check on the power of the Monarch. One can be quite sure that, were Britain to have an elected president, no such restraints would operate.

The political role of the Monarchy has therefore become more important, and not less, since Bagehot's day. While the more bright-eyed and unthinking of our Parliament-arians might believe that it would suit their careers better if they had a system more like that of the French or the Germans or the Italians, there are many (not least, Germans, Italians and French) who would dispute their cosy view of democratic systems and see virtues in the British system which are perhaps not apparent to those who have come to take it for granted.

The virtue of the system and the fact that everyone takes it for granted are very much part of Elizabeth II's manner of conducting herself. She has been unobtrusive and conscientious for so long that people suppose that the 'machine' of Monarchy works smoothly almost as an act of nature. This is not so. We only notice machines when they begin to malfunction. The smoothness with which the monarchical machine has operated is a measure of the Queen's tremendous skill.

There are now two major threats to the smooth running of the machine; for the sake of shorthand one could describe them as her mother and her children.

Not, of course, that Her Majesty the Queen Mother has been anything but a pillar of the Monarchy, nor that the Queen's children, as individuals and in their own sphere, are not all perfectly decent individuals. But the Queen Mother's way of being a Queen, which in some measure Queen Elizabeth II has tried to imitate, while appropriate for wartime Britain, is out of step with the times. As a

matter of habit, lord mayors, lords-lieutenant, chairmen
of companies and managers of hospitals will continue to
bombard Buckingham Palace with requests that the Queen
should come to open this, unveil that; a scurrying parody
of her parents, who moved from bomb-site to bomb-site
during the Second World War to rally the spirits of their
people. People in modern Britain do not need their spirits
rallying in quite this way, and the programme of Royal
visits (which, candidly, few would miss if they stopped)
has set up in the public mind the wholly false idea that
this is the Queen's 'job': going round and unveiling things
and opening things. It is also deemed in some journalistic
quarters to be the 'job' of other members of the Royal
Family too, and individuals such as Princess Margaret,
who has quite understandably played down this aspect of
life as much as possible in recent years, are taken to task
if they do not perform these useless and rather ridiculous
functions.

The Queen does not have a 'job', though the Crown has
a function. Now that they have nearly all been removed
from the Civil List,* none of the Queen's relations is obliged
to perform any public functions whatsoever. This is something which the Queen Mother would go to her grave
misunderstanding. Edward VIII caused mortal offence on
September 23, 1936, by sending the Duke and Duchess
of York (the future George VI and Queen Elizabeth) to
open a hospital in Aberdeen. The local dignitaries had
hoped that the King would open the hospital, but he went
instead, quite publicly, to the railway station to welcome
Mrs Simpson on her visit to Balmoral.† To show that she
was never to be accused of putting pleasure before duty,

*See Chapter Nine.
†Philip Ziegler, *King Edward VIII* (1990) p.288.

the Queen Mother spent the next sixty years of her life opening hospitals, and she groomed her children to do the same. But no one felt as strongly as she did about her brother-in-law's alleged offence, and those who did feel strongly have forgiven him by now. Royal personages do not have to be visible all the time; they do not even have to be seen doing good. Bagehot was right to say that it cheers us all up to read of Princes going to race meetings.

To be so much in public has done the Queen no harm, but hers has been a discreet and largely blameless life. Unfortunately for her children, they have all survived into an age where newspapers believe that public personages deserve perpetual public scrutiny, even on occasions when they would prefer to be private.

The longer her reign has continued, the more forceful have seemed the criticisms of Lord Altrincham in 1957. While she has continued to be a conscientious Monarch, cast very firmly in the mould of her father and grandfather, she has allowed herself to be advised and surrounded by persons whom Altrincham castigated as 'tweedy'. In times when everything is progressing smoothly, there is nothing wrong with these 'tweedy', slightly stuffy courtiers. But, because they were presumably so much out of sympathy with the social and political developments of the twentieth century, they have been powerless to protect the Queen against the cruellest assaults of the Press. Her Press Secretaries have tended to be gentlemen when they should have been bruisers, poachers turned gamekeepers who knew the world of tabloid journalism from the inside. While Mrs Thatcher appointed Bernard Ingham as her Press Secretary – a bruiser if ever there was one – the Queen, at the darkest hour of her *annus horribilis*, had Sir Robert Fellowes, a man who was bamboozled by his sister-in-law the Princess of Wales simply because he was too nice.

At the same time, because she is so unmodern that she does not even know what it is to be modern, the Queen has allowed herself to be guided by those who suggested that the Royal Family should 'modernise' itself. Her late mentor, Lord Mountbatten, was the chief offender in this area, but Prince Philip, Mountbatten's nephew, must probably shoulder some of the blame too. One of Prince Philip's most devoted biographers, Tim Heald, congratulates his subject for 'nursing the Royal Family into the twentieth century'.* That Prince Philip has made this part of his life's work is not in question, but it remains questionable whether the late-twentieth century is a very good habitat for any Royal Family, let alone the House of Windsor. As a conscientious (but always, one suspects, slightly stiff) mother – one recollects the occasion when she flew home from some foreign tour to greet the six-year-old Prince Charles by shaking his hand – she has wanted to involve her children in 'The Firm'. This idea of 'The Firm' was manageable when it consisted merely of the King, the Queen, Lilibet and Margaret Rose. It is a little less easy to see what possible Royal functions could be found for four children, their spouses, their children and all the cousins. Many of them, even remote relations by marriage such as the Duchess of Kent, have done their best, opening hospitals as if there was no tomorrow. But the price paid for all this dutifulness is that any member of the Queen's family seems like fair game to the tabloid papers; and when taken as a whole, the Royal Family are seen (from a strictly constitutional perspective) to be so useless that the institution of Monarchy itself is useless.

*Tim Heald, *The Duke* (1991) p.253.

It has to be said – not as a value judgement but as a matter of fact – that none of the Queen's children makes a very obvious heir to the throne. The position of Prince Charles has already been discussed. The Princess Royal has done sterling work as the President of the Save the Children Fund, but her marital position makes it impossible that she could ever be the Supreme Governor of the Church of England, and she has made it very clear, by moving out of Royal residences even when in London and renting a flat in Dolphin Square, that she does not wish to be considered as an active member of 'The Firm'. At the time of writing, Prince Andrew's marital position would also make it very embarrassing for him to inherit the Throne – which only leaves Prince Edward, who has so far had no marital difficulties, perhaps because nature has blessed him with a disinclination towards matrimony. There is no reason to suppose that he would make a bad King, but it has seemed for the last few years as though he would prefer a career in the theatre.

Sir Henry Marten had a conscientious young pupil. She learnt how to be a Monarch, and she has performed the role so flawlessly that anyone who comes after her will seem second-rate. But the position is rather more serious than that. Because of what has happened in the last few years, there can never be a Monarch quite in Elizabeth II's mould. The Bagehot formula will not work for any of her children, however they contort themselves and try to fit themselves into it. They can never be regarded as exemplars, nor as religious icons, nor as ideals of daily life, and none of them looks exactly the sort of which sage political counsellors are made. The Queen's last function must be to live a very long time, until some new Bagehot arises to advise her successors how the Monarchy might survive. Otherwise, we must feel ourselves close not merely to the decline, but to the end, of the House of Windsor.

SIX

The House of Windsor and the Press

'Most journalists just want the shot
where you're seen picking your nose.'

Prince Philip in Douglas Keay, *Elizabeth II*

Relations between the House of Windsor and the British Press have, until a decade ago, been distant and polite. It was traditionally left to the foreign newspapers and broadcasting stations to intrude or to criticise. From 1910 until 1980, most journalistic comment on the Royal House in Britain bordered on the sycophantic, and newspaper coverage of Royal events was little better than an extended or illustrated version of the Court Circular, published each day by the various courts and households of the Royal Family, chronicling their public doings and arrangements, the appointments of lords and ladies-in-waiting, the attendance at receptions, the representation of Royal personages by the attendance of someone else at memorial services. 'KENSINGTON PALACE, February 17th, The Princess Margaret, Countess of Snowdon, was represented by The Lady Sarah Armstrong-Jones at a service of thanksgiving for the life of

Sir Kenneth MacMillan in Westminster Abbey today . . .' 'BUCKINGHAM PALACE, February 8th, The Lady Elton has succeeded the Lady Susan Hussey as Lady-in-Waiting to the Queen.' And, stop press!, 'CLARENCE HOUSE,* February 17th, Queen Elizabeth the Queen Mother, Honorary Colonel, The Royal Yeomanry, this evening opened Cavalry House, the new Regimental Headquarters at the Duke of York's Head-quarters . . .' Can there be anything more reassuring for a conservative-minded Briton than these daily bulletins from the Royal Palaces? Can there be anything more calculated to make him or her feel that the world is as it was, and as it should be?

Even in the 1930s, however, the deference felt for the Crown by the Press was matched by the fear and respect shown by the Crown for the Fourth Estate. Presumably the most extreme example of this is the death of George V itself, which the family arranged very largely with the newspapers in mind. When, on January 20, 1936, it became apparent that the King was dying, a concern was expressed that he might struggle through the night and die after the morning papers had 'gone to bed'. It would therefore have fallen to the evening newspapers in London to convey the news of the King's death to the world. To spare his Royal master this indignity and to ensure that his sovereign's demise should first be reported in *The Times*, Lord Dawson of Penn, Chief Physician to His Majesty, administered a lethal dose of chloroform to George V some time before dinner at Sandringham. He picked up a menu-card from the household dining-room and wrote on it what the royal biographer describes as 'a farewell of classic simplicity': 'The King's life is moving peacefully to its close.' After

---

* The official residence of Queen Elizabeth the Queen Mother.

eating dinner with Queen Mary and her children, Lord Dawson was able to announce the King's death to the Editor of *The Times*. Earlier in the day, when the King was still conscious and a few members of the Privy Council had stood around in his bedroom, Dawson had suggested to His Majesty that, were his health to improve, he might benefit from a visit to his beloved Bognor Regis. This provoked the highly characteristic reply, 'Bugger Bognor!' Since the Royal Household were able to engineer the exact hour of their Sovereign's departure from this world, it is not surprising that they should have also chosen to offer to the world an amended version of George's last words. 'Bugger Bognor' became, in the official version, 'How is the Empire?' Only the most rigorous pedants or seekers after historical exactitude would deny that this was an ingeniously pleasing emendation.

Those who know how highly King George V was regarded by his subjects in the closing years of his reign might be surprised by his wife's caution in the timing of his death and the breaking of the news. But Queen Mary was old enough to remember when relations between the Royal Family and the Press were very much less cordial, and when newspapers contained regular attacks on the institution of Monarchy itself, demands that the Queen be paid less money, and prurient inquiries into the marital troubles of the Prince of Wales. In April 1871, for example, Gladstone remarked gloomily to Lord Palmerston, the Foreign Secretary, that he had been reading *Reynolds's Newspaper*, a popular imprint with a circulation of over 300,000. One item in the paper described the Prince of Wales losing a fortune in the gambling salons of Homburg; another complained of Queen Victoria's parsimony and hoarding of money 'obtained from the toil and sweat of the British working man'. 'Things go from bad to worse,' said Gladstone. 'I see *What Does She Do*

With It? on the walls of the station at Birkenhead.'*

Throughout the nineteenth century the British Press attacked the Monarch and her family for their idleness and greed. Queen Victoria herself formed the view that the institution was so unpopular that it would not outlast her lifetime by more than twenty years. She failed to understand that it was she herself who was unpopular, not the Crown; and as soon as Bertie (whom she considered such a disgrace to the family) became King, the Royal Family became extremely popular, not merely in Great Britain but in the rest of Europe as well.

Queen Victoria's family learnt other lessons from her hostile treatment at the hands of the Press. They knew that they were only protected and kept in their position of privilege by 'the Establishment'. The very undemocratic nature of England meant that no institution could be directly answerable to 'the People' by democratic means. The Members of Parliament are not, in the British system, obliged to reflect the views or wishes of their constituents. They are the representatives of the people, not their unthinking mouthpiece. As figures who to some extent are part of the Establishment, and to some extent depend upon it, they are very unlikely ever to criticise the Crown. There are always one or two Members of Parliament in any one generation who take it upon themselves to do this, but they almost instantaneously become 'joke' figures (if they were not joke figures to start with). Until the present Parliament (that convened after the 1992 election), those who intended to have a serious political career in Britain have not dared to criticise the Monarchy. Things are beginning to alter now, but until recently it has meant that when criticism of the Monarch or the institution of Monarchy has been made,

*Christopher Hibbert, *Edward VII* (1976) p.111.

it has been left to the Press alone to fulfil this democratic role; and, given the nature of matters in Britain, it is not a role which, historically, the Press has fulfilled with any great relish. Indeed, for the greater part of the twentieth century, the English newspapers, when compared with their Victorian or Regency counterparts, have been almost incredibly diffident and mealy-mouthed.

The year which followed the death of King George V was perhaps the most dramatic in the history of the British Monarchy, but not a whisper of what was taking place was ever reported at the time to the British people. Newspaper readers in the United States and on the European continent were kept abreast – with the degree of journalistic inaccuracy which was to be expected in such a situation – with the King's Matter. Edward VIII was enamoured of Mrs Simpson; he intended to marry her; this was regarded by the Prime Minister, by the Archbishop of Canterbury and by the Prime Ministers of the Dominions as entirely unacceptable. Abdication was an inevitability. And yet it was not until a week before the Abdication occurred that the story of Edward and Mrs Simpson appeared in the English Press. Journalists are rightly mocked for repeating the cliché that the public has 'the right to know' this or that; G. K. Chesterton, that great journalist who died in the same year as the Abdication, was probably closer to the truth when he said that journalism was the art of interesting people in the fact that Lady Jones was dead who had not heard that Lady Jones had ever been alive. But, in the case of the Abdication, there surely was a case for saying that the People had 'a right to know'.

The reason for the silence of the papers was that the proprietors had been frightened off by the Establishment – at this date it still made sense to speak of such a thing. The Establishment had decided, long before the 'Abdication crisis', that they would get rid of the King, and they did not wish their plans – for the coronation of the Duchess of York and their tame King-candidate, her husband – to be interfered with by a popular upsurge. Had the Abdication crisis happened in the atmosphere of 1992, with a free Press all commenting on the situation and influencing events as they unfolded, it is difficult to know what would have happened, but it is easy to picture how some of the newspapers would have reacted. Some would have sided openly with Mrs Simpson. Others would have adopted the 'Hands off our King!' approach. In any event, it is hard to suppose that the Abdication would have happened quietly and behind closed doors. Apart from anything else, Edward VIII's frequent cross-Channel telephone calls with his future Duchess would have been intercepted by the Intelligence services and sold to the highest bidder. There might have been a surge of republicanism which would have led to the abolition of the Monarchy. There might, instead, have been a populist movement to crown Queen Wallis in Westminster Abbey: a consequence which traditionalists might have abhorred more than the abolition of the Monarchy itself. But the Press was muzzled in 1936, and so neither thing happened. Instead, King George VI and Queen Elizabeth were crowned, and their elder daughter Lilibet was groomed for becoming the Queen of England.

There were by now quite a lot of skeletons hanging in their family cupboard; by the end of the war, during which a high proportion of the King's German relatives had been active and keen Nazis, there were even more. So it is not surprising that Queen Elizabeth and King George developed an attitude to the Press which was almost paranoid. Anything except 'official' reporting was frowned upon. Queen Elizabeth, an adept at inventing new Royal traditions, coined the idea (unknown to Pepys, Horace Walpole, Greville, Creevey,

Disraeli et al.) that no loyal subjects ever repeated what was said to them by a member of the Royal Family. The price paid for indiscretion was immediate ostracism from the Royal circle, as any ex-friend of Queen Elizabeth's (there are many) could attest.

The legend of the Forbidden Fruit is habitually repeated in life, as in folk-tale. The tree from which you must not eat, the cupboard which you must never open – these are the ones which prove too tempting for the unfortunate protagonists of any tale. The employees of Queen Elizabeth enjoyed many freedoms, except the freedom to repeat what was said by their Royal employers. It was a restriction which the governess to the Little Princesses, Marion Crawford, found intolerable.

Crawfie, as the girls called her, was not a seditious communist intent upon bringing down the government. Nor was she motivated by greed, though there is no doubt that she made some money out of her written account of the childhood of Lilibet and Margaret Rose, *The Little Princesses*. Friends and courtiers of the Queen Mother believe that Crawfie wrote *The Little Princesses* out of pique because she was not made a Dame Commander of the Victorian Order for her services to the Royal Household.* To Queen Elizabeth, who has been so dominated by a desire for revenge,† this might seem a plausible motive for writing a book, but to those of a more equable disposition it will be obvious how seldom human beings outside the walls of Clarence House, or the more lurid pages of literature, are ever motivated purely by a desire for revenge. Crawfie was not Prince Hamlet or the Count of Monte Cristo: she was that much more innocent and dangerous thing, a compulsive

---

* Elizabeth Longford, *Elizabeth R* (1977) p.117.
† i.e. revenge on Wallis Simpson for marrying King Edward VIII.

blabbermouth. She had been the witness to the upbringing of the future Queen of England and her sister. She retained for them the toadyish worship, entirely devoid of irony, without which it is impossible to endure the company of any Royal personage for more than an evening. But her tongue was stronger than her heart. She could not resist *telling*.

Like the real village gossip she was, Crawfie could not resist bringing everything in: the Emperor of India dies, and it is an occasion for Crawfie to remember her own toothache. But, buried in the artless, syrupy prose, there are unforgettable vignettes of both the little girls – prophetic snapshots of what they were and what they were to become.

'I had a telegram almost immediately asking me to return to Royal Lodge, Windsor, where the children were. I had had a tooth out the day before. Cocaine never goes through my face; it sat there like an apple on my cheek, and I looked as though I had been crying my eyes out. I can still remember the sort of hush that had fallen over England. All the way down south the stations were strangely silent and empty, and everyone looked sad. People had not realised how much they loved the old King until he was dead.

'At Royal Lodge two little figures were waiting for me. The Duke and Duchess had gone to town and left a message for me: "Don't let all this depress them more than is absolutely necessary, Crawfie. They are so young."

'I kept them in Windsor until all arrangements had been made for the funeral, then I took them to London. Margaret was much too young to pay attention to what was going on. She was intrigued by the fact that Alah [their nurse] from time to time burst into a flood of tears.

'Lilibet in her sensitive fashion felt it all deeply. It was very touching to see how hard she tried to do what she felt was expected of her. I remember her pausing doubtfully as she groomed one of the toy horses and looking up at me for a moment.

' "Oh, Crawfie . . . ought we to play?" she asked . . .

'I remember I was very bothered at the thought of Lilibet going to the lying-in-state. She was so young, I thought. What could she possibly know of death? But she had to go. She drove off with the Duke and Duchess, in her black coat and black velvet tammie, looking very small and, I thought, rather scared . . .

' "Uncle David* was there," she told me afterwards, "and he never moved at all, Crawfie. Not even an eyelid. It was wonderful. And everyone was so quiet. As if the King were asleep." '

And so on, and so on. There is nothing in *The Little Princesses* which is not profoundly respectful towards the Royal Family and gushingly affectionate about Crawfie's young charges. But to have published it at all was regarded as an act of unpardonable sedition, and for ever afterwards the repetition of family intimacies was known as 'doing a Crawfie' – the unpardonable sin in Queen Elizabeth the Queen Mother's eyes.

Writing in 1983, Elizabeth Longford claimed – on the scarcely reliable evidence of her friend and neighbour Malcolm Muggeridge – that *The Little Princesses* had in fact been written by the biographer of George V, Harold Nicolson. This is quite a good joke about Nicolson, who had his governessy side, but it is not to be taken seriously. In real life, the Royal Family had no doubt at all about the authenticity of *The Little Princesses*, and Crawfie was cruelly ostracised. That peculiarly harsh and unforgiving streak in the Queen Mother, which allowed her brother-in-law to be banished for a lifetime, moved equally swiftly to destroy

*The future Duke of Windsor.

Crawfie. Lilibet and Margaret Rose were never to see or speak to their old governess again.

'Royal control on memoirs has been decidedly tightened since the Crawford best-seller,' Lady Longford wrote. This was a polite understatement. The Royal Family exercised an iron control over what was written about them; their capacity for censorship would have been the envy of Stalin's Politburo; and this applied not merely to what journalists or others said about the *living*, but to what scholars said about the dead. Any serious historian wishing to write books which touch on Royal history is obliged to use the Royal archives at Windsor. Access to this archive is far from free. It has to be worked for. If the archivist and her assistants suspect a scholar of any mischievous intent, he or she will certainly be excluded from the archives.

Any Royal biographer will tell you that fierce censorship is operated by the Royal archives, even if the material relates to events which happened a hundred or more years ago. An acquaintance of mine, researching the Royal family in the nineteenth century, was astonished to discover in the archives at Windsor the draft of a letter written by Prince Albert in 1861 to the Privy Council. It was written shortly after the death of his mother-in-law. Queen Victoria had in effect taken leave of her senses and was hysterical much of the time. Life with her had become unendurable. The letter was asking, should the Queen become permanently insane, whether the Prince Consort could be granted a separation from her.

The scholar who told me of this document's existence implored me not to say anything about it, since, if it ever came out that he was the person who had spoken of it, his entire professional future as a Royal biographer would be jeopardised; he would certainly be forbidden any further access to the archives at Windsor. I asked another royal scholar first whether his fears were justified, and second whether such a document as the Prince Albert letter might not conceivably exist. I received the reply that first he was right – to tell the world that the dear Prince Consort was not happily married would constitute 'doing a Crawfie', even though the parties concerned had all been dead for nearly a century. The Queen did not like her family linen being washed in public – even the antique linen. On the second question, the scholar whom I approached said that such a document could conceivably have existed but, once I had written about it publicly in a newspaper (which I had done), it was almost certain that some discreet hand at Windsor would have found the offending piece of paper and consigned it to the flames.

Some years ago I asked Lady Longford, herself an esteemed historian, biographer and friend of the Royal Family, why they were quite so fearful. After all, I said, the Vatican itself, which had (one would have supposed) far more dangerous secrets to hide, is more liberal than Windsor Castle. When Owen Chadwick wished to investigate the Papal archives for that most delicate of periods, the Second World War, he received no opposition at all. The then Pope, Paul VI, had not read all the documents in the files of his predecessor Pius XII. It was being widely suggested, on no evidence, that the wartime Pope had behaved discreditably during the war, either by not doing enough to speak out against the Nazis or even by nursing secret sympathy for them. No one knew, until the files were open, the truth or otherwise of these highly damaging allegations. And yet no restrictions whatsoever were placed upon Owen Chadwick. Though Chadwick was not a Catholic, he was allowed to read anything he liked and to draw any conclusions which he chose.

When I said this to Lady Longford, who is a devout

Catholic, she admitted that there was a difference of approach between the Roman Pontiff and the English Monarch. 'But then, you see,' she said, 'the Pope really does believe that he has been given the keys of the kingdom, and that the gates of hell cannot prevail against him. No such assurance has ever been given to the English Kings and Queens. It is understandable that they should be a little more cautious.'

Some would think that they took caution to the point of mania. Certainly, in the post-Crawfie era, there was such an atmosphere of reverence surrounding the Royal Family and household that the merest breath of criticism, however mild, was treated in Great Britain with some of the horror which is aroused by blasphemy in countries of the Islamic world. The case of Lord Altrincham is a good example.

The 1960s certainly changed the atmosphere of stultifying sycophancy which surrounded the Queen. The satirical magazine *Private Eye* reverted to robustly eighteenth-century satires on the Monarch and her family. The Queen was referred to as Brenda, and her sister as Yvonne – somehow, these appellations are perfect. 'True-Life Romances' in the manner of cheap women's magazines were composed (allegedly by the author Sylvie Krin) about the emotional lives of Brenda's children. *Love in the Saddle*, about Princess Anne, was a personal favourite of mine, though the one which achieved classic status was the story of the Prince of Wales and his marriage – *Heir of Sorrows* – which eventually had to be discontinued since life so doggedly continued to imitate art, and the Prince in particular began to behave more and more in the way that *Private Eye* depicted him, rather as if he were a puppet, mouthing lines written for him by Sylvie Krin.

Addicts of a crueller form of Royal satire will treasure the fantasies of Auberon Waugh in his famous Diaries.

His physical revulsion against Princess Anne is perhaps one of the most savage things about these productions. On January 23, 1978, he noted that 'the Queen was most interested in some photographs which I showed her from today's *Daily Express*: of a Saudi-Arabian commoner being beheaded after his wife, a princess, had been shot for daring to marry him. But she was not in the least bit amused when I started making pointed remarks about her own son-in-law Captain Mark Phillips and his bride, Princess-Dame Anne Phillips.' The diary pretends that Waugh is on intimate terms with all the Windsors. 'For over a month now I haven't heard a squeak from any member of the Royal Family. I was beginning to wonder why they were avoiding me, but today everything is explained. Prince Michael of Kent (whom I have not seen since he was a reasonably attractive junior boy at Eton) announces his plans to marry the Catholic wife of poor old Tom Troubridge. No wonder they are trying to make themselves scarce.' In the diaries, Waugh adopts the persona of a Catholic squire, very much the Royal Family's social superior (Prince Charles calls him 'Sir'), and the Queen is constantly asking his advice. Indeed, in the fantasy world of the Diaries, Auberon Waugh occupies the same sort of position in the Queen's life as was occupied by Lord Melbourne or the Duke of Wellington in the life of Queen Victoria, only with the difference that between the present Queen and Waugh there is rather more physical intimacy. Though they are not lovers, they enjoy stroking each other's feet while he offers her his advice on issues of the day.

Perhaps the most prophetic entry in the Diaries concerning the Monarchy and the Press is that for November 28, 1980. It was at the time of Prince Charles's courtship, and a story had appeared in the *Sunday Mirror* to the effect that the Prince had spent the night in a railway siding, alone in a deserted Royal train with Diana Spencer. 'I never thought I would find myself jumping to the defence of Bob Edwards, curly-headed editor of the *Sunday Mirror*, but things are getting serious. Bob's resignation from the Kennel Club may be at stake if senior stewards have their way after his clash with Buckingham Palace over whether or not Prince Charles was romancing late at night with his beloved on the Royal Train. I was not there and so have an open mind on the crucial point of whether or not any romancing took place. But nobody can sit back idly and see a respected public figure like Bob Edwards – whose position does not allow him to hit back – have his name dragged through the mud by such proven liars as inhabit Buckingham Palace . . . If the Queen is tired of "press lies" as she informed the *Daily Telegraph*, then it is plain she is tired and ought to abdicate.'

By the time *Private Eye* had been in production for ten or fifteen years, television had developed its 'satirical' view of Royalty to a position where gentle mockery gave place to scabrous lampoon. The puppets on *Spitting Image* showed the Royal Family as ugly and contemptible. The Queen Mother was portrayed as a gin-sodden old Cockney, frequently applying the bottle to her lips. The Duchess of York was even seen in a recent episode undergoing colonic irrigation. That such programmes have appeared on television and gradually been accepted as part of the common hoard of mass-culture 'jokes' makes the older style of reverence for the Royal Family seem almost unthinkable today. I noticed this in a very minor way when Her Majesty the Queen Mother was ninety years old and I published (in a small weekly magazine) an account of meeting her at dinner some years before. Perhaps a few more copies of this small-circulation paper were sold in consequence, but it did not really produce outrage (except in my host on the occasion of the dinner) that I had broken with Royal protocol and repeated what was said to me by the Queen Mother. It was all harmless stuff – but then, so had Altrincham and Malcolm Muggeridge been harmless. Older journalists, when I printed my conversation with the Queen Mother, said that I would receive the same sort of treatment and could expect a few brickbats to come my way. They could not have been more wrong. It was a small sign of how things had changed. My article made very little more impact than if I were describing a meeting with a famous film star who did not normally give interviews.

One of the great changes which I have noticed personally in the last few years in London is the nature of Royal tittle-tattle among journalists. Until very recently – the last couple of years – rumours and stories about the Royal Family have been very distinctly 'at one remove' from the principal participants. A few Royal gossips have always been in the habit of chatting to some of their journalistic friends, but none of this information was 'authorised', and therefore none of it ever appeared in the newspapers. In 1982, at least ten years before the Princess of Wales had announced her desire to be separated from Prince Charles, Nigel Dempster, the Diarist for the *Daily Mail* and a close personal confidant of 'the Royal moles', had disclosed in his column that all was not well with the Waleses' marriage and that the Princess's displays of distress and bad temper had earned her the title of a 'fiend and a monster' among the more staid courtiers and royalties. In the years which followed, one heard a whole string of stories, about Prince Charles, his wife, his brothers and his sister, not one of which appeared in the newspapers.

Then came the *annus horribilis*. When the 'revelations'

began to appear in the newspapers, there was a predictable outcry from such figures as back-bench Tory MPs, calling for a gag to be put upon the newspapers which printed them. Largely as a result of the 'intrusions' into the Royal Family, a special Commission was established to investigate the extent to which the Press were abusing their freedoms and to explore the possibility of new legislation which would limit the power of journalists to intrude into private lives. At the same time as the *Sunday Times* began its serialisation of Andrew Morton's book, *Diana: Her True Story*, the Press Complaints Commission issued a condemnation, stating that the book was 'dabbling in the stuff of other people's souls'. This was in June 1992.

What surprised me about Morton's book, when it first appeared, was that there was nothing in it which my expert friends, such as Nigel Dempster, had not been openly discussing over the lunch-table for years. In other words, for anyone 'in the know' it was not the contents but the timing which were a puzzle; and the protests by the Press Complaints Commission did not quite seem to hit their target. Like most people, however, the real answer to the mystery – 'Why now?' – had not dawned on me because it was so completely improbable, namely that the book had in effect been 'ghosted' by Mr Morton at the Princess of Wales's dictation.

In fact, for a year or so previous to Morton's book, something quite new had been happening in the newspapers. At the time of the Princess's thirtieth birthday, for example, there was widespread criticism of Prince Charles because he had not left his country house in order to be with his wife in London. On July 2, 1991, the *Daily Mail* carried the headline CAUSE FOR CONCERN, and a story by Nigel Dempster which revealed that the Prince had in fact offered his wife a birthday celebration, and she had turned him down. The next day, in the *Sun*, Andrew Morton had a story in which the Princess supposedly said that she had not wished to have a grand ball with her husband's 'stuffy friends'. 'I had hoped my husband knew me well enough to understand that I don't like that sort of thing,' she said.

Reading this at the time, one assumed that, like the majority of 'Royal' stories to appear in the newspapers, it was, if not straight fabrication, at least a creative reconstruction of the kind of thing the Princess might have said. By the time Mr Morton's book had been published, a year later, one realised that something much odder was at work. The initial 'leak' – that the Prince of Wales had wanted to give a party for his wife – had come direct from the Prince himself. The explanation for her refusal had come direct from the Princess herself. From now onwards, an extraordinary war was waged in print between the Prince and his wife, each using journalists whom they felt they could trust to bring the other into ridicule and contempt. Nearly all the stories printed in the British Press about the Prince and Princess of Wales – stories about the Prince's supposed intimacy with his friend Mrs Parker-Bowles, about the Princess's eating disorders, about the quarrels which they had, with each other and with the Queen and Prince Philip – were printed, not because of the indiscretion of some eagle-eyed reporter, but because of their own conscious decision to 'go public'. And this was a game which they both played. It was not the Princess alone who did it, and at this distance it would be rather difficult to establish which of the royal pair 'started it'. Auberon Waugh's *Private Eye* joke-fantasy, in which royalties treat journalists as confidants and the Royal Family bamboozle the innocent tabloid journalists with their devious lies, began to look perilously like the truth (though of course this was a story in which there were no innocent parties).

As early as May 1991, at a private dinner in Luxembourg, Lord Rothermere, the Chairman of Associated Newspapers, which publishes the *Daily Mail* and the *Evening Standard*, told Lord McGregor, the Chairman of the Press Complaints Commission, that the Prince and Princess had taken this course of action. His words were that 'the Prince and Princess of Wales had each recruited national newspapers to carry their own accounts of their marital rifts'.*

Now, what is of interest about this confession by Lord McGregor is that, in spite of his knowing the facts of the case, he continued to behave, as Chairman of the Press Complaints Commission, as if the 'intrusions' into the Royal marriage came from journalists alone, rather than being orchestrated by the Royal pair themselves. His reason for doing this was that he had confronted the Queen's Press Secretary, Sir Robert Fellowes (brother-in-law to the Princess of Wales), with what Lord Rothermere had said, and it was categorically denied by Sir Robert. McGregor told Fellowes that he, on behalf of the Royal Family, should send a list of the inaccuracies in Morton's book to the Press Complaints Commission, and each inaccuracy could then be dealt with in turn.

It was clear to any journalist who knew how these things worked that the Morton book, and all the subsequent journalistic 'intrusion' into the Waleses' marriage, could not have happened without authorisation from some Royal quarter. Something new had happened in the course of 1991 which enabled the journalists to print the stories which were beginning to emerge. That new development had to be that Prince Charles and his wife were authorising journalists to tell their stories, since no journalist, no editor and no proprietor would dare to publish

*Letter by Lord McGregor in the *Guardian*, January 12, 1993.

stories of such magnitude unless they had been substantiated.

This fact, obvious to any jobbing journalist, is less obvious to the reading public (however sophisticated), and this was why the Palace was able for so long to represent this seedy episode in Royal history as a sudden invasion of the citadels of civilisation by the barbarian hordes. Everyone in Royal circles knew that Mr Morton's book was substantially true, but this did not prevent them all from attempting to pretend that it was false. One of the known sources for Mr Morton's stories was Carolyn Bartholomew, the Princess of Wales's friend and former flatmate. When the denunciations of Morton were at their height, Lady Diana staged a very public visit to Carolyn Bartholomew's house and k issed her openly as she was greeted on the doorstep. On this occasion, the newspapermen and photographers, sensing that it was a moment of some intimacy between the two friends, held back. Lady Diana, however, surprised them all by driving her car twice round the block, to make sure that her public display of friendship with Mr Morton's sources was immortalised on camera.

The fairly unsubtle code of this occasion was not difficult to crack, either for the Press or for the Palace. Thereafter, it was open war between the official Royal Press Secretaries (including Sir Robert Fellowes) and Lady Diana. When the extent of Palace hypocrisy was finally rumbled in January 1993, and Lord McGregor was forced to admit that both sides in the Waleses' marriage rift had fed the press with stories, it was no surprise that the Prince's party put all the blame on to the Princess. The Princess of Wales had, the public were informed, 'in practice been invading her own privacy'.

This is perfectly true, but it is not, of course, the whole truth. As someone who became an idol of the world's Press from the moment she was engaged to be married, Lady Diana showed an exceptional gift for self-promotion. If the Palace thought that they were able to beat her at her own game, they were disastrously wrong. She quickly mastered the power of the visual image. Outside the complicated realm of economics, nearly all the great twentieth-century news 'stories' have in fact been photographs. When things went right for Lady Diana, she learnt how to be the 'smiling Princess'. But when she felt the Court and her husband's friends and family were conspiring against her, she knew that she could – at least for a time – promote a picture of herself to the world which told its own story, long before any of us necessarily knew about her husband's alleged emotional involvements elsewhere.

One of these was the famous photo opportunity at the Taj Mahal in February 1991. Her husband, on a previous visit to India, had famously said that he would like to take his affianced bride to this monument to married love. Eleven years after he had made this declaration, he was on an official visit to India in the company of this same wife. She chose a day when he was delivering a speech in Delhi – an engagement which he could not possibly cancel at short notice – to travel to the Taj Mahal to be photographed alone. All her aides and staff were banished from the picture, and she was photographed there, a solitary figure, neglected by her indifferent husband. The photographic message was clear, and it had the added amusement value that once again she had 'upstaged' her husband. His speech in Delhi received scant attention in the next morning's newspapers.

She staged a similar photographic message to the world in May, when she posed alone at the Pyramids during an official visit to Egypt. Charles had come out to Egypt with her, but then left her there alone to travel on to Turkey where, as we subsequently learned, he met up with Mrs Parker-Bowles. (When this fact was disclosed by Charles's biographer Anthony Holden in the February 1993 edition of *Vanity Fair*, it was vigorously denied by the Prince's representatives, speaking through the medium of Nigel Dempster in the *Daily Mail*. But Charles did in fact go to Turkey on that occasion in order to be with Mrs Parker-Bowles.)*

In general, men tend to like – or besottedly to adore – Lady Diana, and for that very reason women tend not to like her. Since journalism is one of the few professions in which there is a more or less equal proportion of men and women working at a high level, it is not surprising that a diversity of views have suggested themselves to the commentators about Lady Diana's so-called 'manipulation' of the media. Some journalists have felt inclined to comment upon its morality. What is not in doubt is its boldness.

It certainly seems as if Lady Diana may have connived at the 'press intrusions into her private life' as a means of releasing herself from her husband. This is a measure of how powerful the Press had become in the Royal Story. Until the arrival of Lady Diana in the family, the Royals – even the indiscreet ones – behaved with tremendous circumspection in relation to their journalist 'contacts' or friends. Any journalist who abused the trust of a member of the Royal Family knew that he or she would never be admitted into Royal circles again, so it simply was not worth the while of any seasoned Royal-watcher or Court Correspondent to quote Royal stories unless they were supplied 'on the record'. This meant that almost all Royal news and almost all Royal books, with the exception of Crawfie's, were stultifyingly boring, because they only told us what the Royal Family wanted us to know.

*Private information.

Lady Diana saw that, by 'doing a Crawfie', she could exercise enormous power over her husband and his family. Only they would know fully how much of Andrew Morton's book was true. The rest of us could only guess. This left her in a position of great strength when her lawyers came to approach her husband's lawyers, in the summer of 1992, to discuss the possibility of a marital separation.

While these negotiations were in progress, 'The Redhead', as Lady Diana contemptuously called the Duchess of York, had decided that she too would like to clamber aboard the bandwagon. If Diana could tell the story of her marriage to the Press, why shouldn't she? With the help of her friend, the Texan millionaire John Bryan, she entered into negotiations with the *Daily Mail* with a view to publishing her 'story'. Realising that they were on to a very hot thing, the *Mail* had been deliberately restrained about its reporting of the Duchess's marital troubles, and had never made use of its knowledge that John Bryan was extremely close to the Duchess.

Unfortunately for both the *Mail* and the Duchess, events were to pass out of their hands. Though estranged from her husband Andrew, she accompanied him up to Balmoral with their two daughters. And it was during the week that they were there that the *Daily Mirror* published what must be some of the most remarkable Royal portraits ever to appear in a British newspaper. *Paris-Match*, which bought the rights in these interesting glimpses of a Royal holiday, have subsequently paid a substantial sum of money in legal damages both to the Duchess and to her financial adviser. Everyone agreed that it was morally insupportable that such photographs should be in circulation, and everyone in Great Britain bought the *Daily Mirror* on the morning that they were published. The scene at Balmoral on the morning when the newspaper was published may only be imagined. It would certainly need another pen than mine to reconstruct the conversations, if any, which took place between the Duchess and her husband's family before she took a speedy flight to London on an ordinary shuttle from Aberdeen that day. Her position is irrecoverable, the more so since the revelations of Miss Player, concerning that lady's love affair with Her Royal Highness's father, Major Ferguson. But the Duchess of York and her sordid life, though of entertainment value in the cheaper newspapers, does not have a serious part to play in this story, except in so far as she contributed to the general cheapening of the Royal House in the eyes of the Press. And, doubtless, whenever she pops up in the tabloids, she will continue to do so for many entertaining years to come.

But what of the serious implications of the last few years? Does the present relationship between the Press, particularly the British Press, and Buckingham Palace represent a threat to the institution of Monarchy itself?

In a leader of December 19, 1992, the Conservative newspaper the *Daily Telegraph* asked whether the Monarchy had a future. Having rehearsed the marital troubles of the Prince of Wales, it claimed that 'the future of the Prince of Wales and of the Monarchy as a whole will depend upon the behaviour of those concerned *and the public response to them* [my italics] over the next generation, rather than upon any narrow technical interpretation of the constitution'. The leader continues, 'The most serious threat to the Monarchy's future stems not from the few who are directly hostile to it, but from the growing number who are indifferent. Vociferous critics have argued in the past week that the Royal Family is irrelevant to modern British life. Many of the young, especially, do not feel the awe and respect which the Royal Family has traditionally attracted. They simply do not care. It is this generation whose support and enthusiasm are needed to secure the Monarchy's future in the 21st century.'

This article would appear to be seriously meant, and the 'arguments' which it advances are frequently heard on British lips at the present time. The argument is that the Monarch is only there on sufferance. This, historically speaking, has been true. But what is new is the name of the supposed master calling the Monarch's tune. James II and Edward VIII were both fired, as William III and George I had been hired, by the same master – the oligarchy who ruled Britain at the time – which could variously be described as the aristocracy, the Establishment or both. Now that the Establishment has been dissolved in real terms, it is very hard to see who has the power to hire and fire Monarchs. But we can see who think they have this power: the Press barons and, beneath the barons, the newspaper editors.

This is surely the new development in the life of the Royal Family, and the one which is, from everyone's point of view except that of the journalists, the most damaging to the Monarchy. Examine the *Telegraph*'s argument in more detail: it is one which one hears repeated week in, week out, in any editorial conference in London where newspaper editors freely and grandly speak of which members of the Royal Family they will 'allow' to continue, and which they will 'get rid of', 'destroy', etc.

The Royal Family is 'irrelevant to modern life' – whatever this is supposed to mean. Certain members of it are in danger of failing to behave in a way which 'society' will accept. The future of the Monarchy apparently depends upon the support of the younger generation of uneducated people with no sense of the past. 'Part of the Monarchy's problem is that the Monarchy is strongly associated with the past, with an historical legacy about which young people ignorant of the dates of Trafalgar and Waterloo know and care less and less.'

Historically, the *Daily Telegraph*'s view is complete nonsense, as any survey of English history would show. Not since the most primitive times of tribal Saxon kingship in the sixth or seventh century has English or British Monarchy been elective, or dependent upon a common consensus. During the last two hundred years there have been two huge constitutional crises when the Crown appeared to be heading for a clash with Parliamentary processes – in 1831–2 and in 1910. In both cases, remarkably enough, the crisis was largely averted by the Sovereign himself. In neither case was the King concerned a clever person in ordinary worldly terms, but both William IV and George V had a basic instinct of common sense and a firm idea of what the constitutional position of the Monarchy was. It existed, and exists, in symbiotic relation to the Houses of Parliament, and it used to exist in a similar symbiosis *vis-à-vis* the upper class or the oligarchy which actually controlled those two institutions of Lords and Commons. What it never did was exist by common consent or democracy. A democratic Monarchy is probably a contradiction in terms. Whether it is or it isn't, no foresight is required in today's world to see who would step forward as the Tribunes of the People, declaring when or whether the monarch must *go*.

The Royal Family's view of the Press until very recent times has tended to be wary, if not paranoid. Prince Philip – with his frequent cry, if the Press cameras come too close, of 'Don't jostle the Queen!' – has been the most outspoken enemy of the popular journalists, whom he describes as the apes of Gibraltar. Reporters approaching Prince Philip in a spirit of polite deference have frequently been told to 'Fuck off' – and this robust attitude to the Press has been inherited by his daughter Princess Anne. It is surely no coincidence that, through all the vicissitudes of the Royal Family's reputation, these two members of it – Prince Philip and Princess Anne – are the ones to whom journalists in general concede a grudging respect. Those who have attempted to woo the Press have had a rougher ride. Dean Inge remarked that he who set out to woo the spirit of the age would soon find himself a widow. This has almost literally occurred with the principal actors in the younger Royal generation, as the separate households and broken marriages of Prince Andrew and Prince Charles both testify. Consequently, the future of the Monarchy is seen to depend neither on parliamentary consensus nor upon constitutional principle, but on the whim of newspaper editors and their journalists. Whether this is a good or bad thing, it certainly changes the function of the Crown as it has been traditionally understood. Disregarding the question of whether it is proper, it also changes the time-scale by which such matters can be considered.

Monarchy is by its nature an old and slow institution. Its place in the scheme of things has been worked out slowly. Prime Ministers and their administrations come and go; the Monarchy remains in place. Its customs, ceremonies and constitutional function provide continuity with the nation's history in a way which no politician could ever do. When Ho Chi Minh was asked whether the French Revolution had brought benefit to the human race, he said that it was too early to say. A similar judgement could be made of the British Monarchy. Its value and function can only be understood on a very long time-scale.

The Press, by contrast, is by definition ephemeral. There is the world of difference between news and history. Most 'news' has a dragonfly life which is dead within a day. Its attitude to everything, including the Royal Family, is instantaneous. It looks for 'stories' which can be hurried on to the front page and which will encourage people to buy newspapers. 'Queen works her way through red boxes for the forty-second year' is hardly a very exciting headline. Nor is: 'Queen meets Prime Minister, as she has done each week for the last forty-odd years, and discusses the future of Canada/Europe/the House of Lords, drawing on a lifetime's constitutional experience.' In the world of hurry and headlines, 'John Sucks Fergie's Toe' or 'Lady Di Throws a Tantrum' make more instantly appealing stories, even though these events, dramatic as they must have seemed at the time, are perhaps of less moment in historical terms.

But this 'perhaps' looks as if it is going to require some readjustment. The new development in the relationship between the Royals and the Press is that, instead of regarding journalists as their enemy, or at the very best a necessary evil, to be kept at arm's length, the Royal Family have decided to woo the media, offering them leaks and stories in the manner of politicians.

Although all this might be seen as 'doing a Crawfie' on a big scale, it has to be admitted that the first person who started on the slippery path of 'publicity' for the Royal House was none other than Her Majesty the Queen. When she had completed her first televised Christmas broadcast, the Queen sighed and said to the producer, 'It's no good, I'm not a film star.'* Unfortunately she, or those who advise her on these matters, had forgotten this fact, and in July 1969 BBC television showed a film called *Royal Family*. It was supposed to be an intimate, behind-the scenes, family snapshot sort of programme. Some indication of the level of public interest shown in the Royal Family may be given

*Douglas Keay, *Elizabeth II* (1991) p. 221.

by the viewing figures: 23 million British people watched it, compared with 30 million who watched the World Cup football final three years earlier, and the 26 or so million people who regularly watched a weekly comedy show called *Steptoe and Son*, about a rag-and-bone merchant.* David Attenborough, a noted BBC film-maker who specialises in the capturing of endangered species on celluloid, was surely right when he said to the producer, 'You know, you're killing the Monarchy with this film you're making. The whole institution depends on mystique and the tribal chief in his hut. If any member of the tribe ever sees inside his hut, then the whole system of the tribal chieftain is damaged and the tribe eventually disintegrates.'† These words sound very wise when read twenty years later.

The point is not merely that the viewing public had been shown inside the hut, but, in allowing themselves to appear on television in this light, the Windsors had become the mere creatures of television. There is no political theory, no *realpolitik*, no system of religious self-abnegation which is more humiliating for individuals than to make them into television 'personalities'. Television is the great leveller, and it quite indiscriminately devours those whom it attracts. Journalists, comedians, orators, great actors might be tempted, by avarice or vanity, to make appearances on it. However brilliant they might be, they become in the shortest possible time indistinguishable from the air-heads on the chat shows, and even from the puppets and cartoon creations of children's TV. The Queen's children did not help matters, when they grew up, by appearing on television fairly frequently. Prince Charles has made two or three documentary films. His brothers and sister-in-law

* Keay, Ibid. p. 224.
† Ibid. p.125.

starred in what must be the most embarrassing Royal appearance in history, including raucous team games in which they wore supposedly funny mediaeval costumes, and Prince Edward, the organiser of the event, flying into a tantrum with the audience for laughing in the wrong places.

Since the Windsors had become 'television personalities', albeit minor ones, it was not surprising that tabloid newspapers should have begun to think that the private lives of the Queen and her family were fair game. Journalists, who had hitherto been forced to make do with the love-life of starlets and stand-up comedians, could now legitimately contemplate the heirs to the throne; and sometimes it was not always easy to tell the difference between them.

In Britain, by the end of 1992, there was a perceptible air of satiety in the reading public. The year concluded with the *Sun* 'leaking' the Queen's Christmas broadcast and printing its contents on the front page two days before Christmas. The Queen was said to be furious, and authorised her solicitor, Sir Matthew Farrer, to sue the newspaper for breach of copyright.

This action was very widely welcomed, because it was felt that the Murdoch press in particular had gone too far in their sadistic and intrusive attacks on the Royal Family. Murdoch or his minions had orchestrated what seemed to be an attack on the Monarchy itself. The *Sun*, edited by Kelvin McKenzie, had published the contents of the 'Squidgygate' tapes. The *Sunday Times* had serialised the Andrew Morton book. In the early months of 1993, Murdoch's Sky TV screened a mini-series based on the break-up of the Waleses' marriage. Few people of the educated class in Britain are able to watch Sky TV since, in order to do so, you have to append a satellite dish on the side of your house. In the still class-ridden society of Britain in 1993, the possession of such a dish would write its owner down as a plebeian. Those sophisticates who did see the film at a private viewing-theatre, sometimes drowned the noise of the characters speaking (or, in the case of the actress playing the Princess of Wales, the noise of being sick) with their contemptuous laughter.

It was still widely believed that Murdoch had not sufficiently received his come-uppance. When accused of megalomania recently, Murdoch is said to have replied that the editor of the *Sun* was more powerful than the Queen. Probably true in modern Britain, but this did not stop a few loyalists from hoping that Her Majesty would fight back. Newspaper magnates could fall as well as rise. Had not Robert Maxwell's empire collapsed about him in ignominy, and was it not true that Murdoch's enterprises were supported by huge borrowing? 1992, with its high interest rates and a continuing world recession, had been an *annus horribilis* for him too. This placed him in a position of some weakness when it came to the flagrant breach of copyright involved in printing the Queen's speech three days early, as if it were an article which she had penned at the behest of that powerful man Kelvin McKenzie. There was talk in Royal circles about the need to hire a tough lawyer, and to pursue Murdoch to the High Courts, taking from him 40 or 50 million pounds.

Unfortunately, the Press got wind of this, and the story appeared in the *Sunday Telegraph*'s 'Mandrake' column, perhaps contributed by that close friend of the Royal family and distinguished royal biographer, Mr Kenneth Rose. Murdoch was on the telephone to his underlings the moment the 'Mandrake' article appeared. The next day, the *Sun* offered a rather perky apology to the Queen, saying that since she had been so kind as to offer to pay income tax they would offer to pay £200,000 to charity. Needless to say, Her Majesty was urged to settle at once.

Many loyalists felt that a great opportunity had been missed. It would obviously have been possible throughout the *annus horribilis* to sue any number of the tabloids for criminal libel. Even the broadsheets spoke openly of Mrs Parker-Bowles in a way which was clearly defamatory, not only of herself and of the Prince of Wales, but of her husband and her children. But no one sued for libel, because no one dared. In a world where bullyism of that kind rules, the Commissions for this and that give advice, and even help draft laws, but the tabloid editors know that they have the Queen and her family on the run. By suing for breach of copyright, the Queen would have avoided any of the embarrassment of a libel case, but could still have exacted punitive damages; but, as always, she was badly advised, and so she will remain the permanent victim of the situation.

Like the stars of proletarian soap operas, the Windsors are doomed to appear in the pages of the cheap papers whenever the editors of those papers cannot think up any proper news; and that will be often. The self-importance of newspaper editors is not to be underestimated, nor is their capacity for self-deception. As someone who works quite happily in the world of newspapers, I have no idea whether or not they are 'influential' or, if so, in what ways they are influential. I should not wish them silenced, even though one might rejoice when the Citizen Kanes have mighty falls. The Royal obsession with the newspapers has become every bit as obsessive as the newspapers' interest in Royalty. Indeed, as we have seen, the Princess of Wales's escape from matrimony was orchestrated by means of the Press. The day-to-day tittle-tattle is not very likely to undermine the constitution. But what Lady Di has done could have wholly destructive effects, for, by publicly humiliating her husband and forcing him to acquiesce in the idea of a divorce, she cuts at the very *raison d'être* of the House of Windsor. For if no one in that family minded about divorce, then the Queen Mother could have remained the Duchess of York all her life (as she claims she would like to have done), bending her knee in gracious curtsies whenever she met her rightful Sovereign Lady, Queen Wallis of Baltimore.

SEVEN

The Merry Wives
of Saxe-Coburg

'We are not supposed to be human.'

Queen Elizabeth (quoted by Crawfie)

'No feeling could seem more childish than the enthusiasm of the English at the marriage of the Prince of
Wales. They treated as a great political event what,
looked at as a matter of pure business, was very small
indeed. But no feeling could be more like common
human nature as it is, and as it is likely to be . . . All
but a few cynics like to see a pretty novel touching
for a moment the dry scenes of the grave world. A
princely marriage is the brilliant edition of a universal
fact, and, as such, it rivets mankind.'

Walter Bagehot, *The English Constitution*

It was a sad day for the Royal Family when Prince Albert
decided that they were meant to be custodians of the
nation's morals. The House of Windsor, the unhappy heirs
of this novel viewpoint, is more than usually haunted by
the difficulties of the married state. In matters of sexual
conduct, it would seem, upon a survey of the last 200 years
of Royal history, as though English Kings and Queens have
veered excessively between extremes of puritanism and
profligacy. Prince Albert, the child of a syphilitic rake and
an adulterous mother who died when he was only twelve
years old, determined to bring up his children with cruel
and puritanical severity. Queen Victoria, the child and
niece of roués and rakes, was only too eager to encourage

him to make the Royal Nursery into the severest of peniten-
tiaries. But, although they made the Prince of Wales (Bertie)
work for hours each day on uncongenial book-learning, and
although they beat him black and blue in an attempt to
inculcate within him the principles of Christian chastity,
he turned out to be just as fat and lewd and sensual as his
grandparents and his obese great-uncles.

Bertie's son, by contrast, was something of a puritan.
Having watched Queen Alexandra, whom he called Mother-
dear (*sic*), suffer as a result of her husband's repeated
adulteries, George V was only too happy to marry Queen
Mary, a figure who was so emotionally buttoned-up that
it is scarcely believable that she was able to proceed with
the necessary preliminaries to pregnancy. That George V's
married life was emotionally or sexually fulfilled, we may
rather doubt – 'marvellous' though Queen Mary was, as
a semi-comic, heroic figure, as a Queen Consort, as a
friend to her husband. Like many puritans before and
since, George V took refuge with the occasional prostitute discreetly arranged for him in seaside towns such
as Bognor – renamed Bognor Regis because of the happy
hours he had spent there. For the rest of the time he was
a rigid upholder of old-fashioned morality. He insisted that
divorced persons should never be admitted to any Royal
function. A Scottish nobleman who had been divorced and
had remarried once pleaded during King George V's reign
with a court functionary at Holyroodhouse in Edinburgh
that his remarriage in church had 'purged' the errors and
sins of the past. 'That may well get you into the Kingdom
of Heaven,' he was told, 'but it will not admit you to the
Palace of Holyroodhouse.' Equally strong was the rule that
divorced persons should not be admitted to the enclosure
at Royal Ascot, an injunction which held good until the
divorce of Princess Margaret in 1978. As for other expres-

sions of human sexuality, they were, in the simple-minded world of George V and Queen Mary, unthinkable. When told that a member of the House of Lords had been involved in a homosexual scandal, George V remarked, 'I always thought people like that shot themselves.' This statement is all the more touching when we remember the emotional complexion of such close relations of the King as his son, the Duke of Kent, and his cousin, Lord Louis Mountbatten.

With innocents like George V and Queen Mary for parents, it was hardly surprising that Edward VIII should have decided to be completely different and to reject what he conceived of as their stodgy values. After that experiment had landed the Royal Family so spectacularly 'in the soup', it was still less surprising that Edward VIII's brother, George VI, and subsequently his niece Elizabeth II, should have been rigid upholders of the George V approach to these matters.

It is no longer any secret that the Queen's own marriage has been far from 'happy' in any of the conventional senses of that term. At the end of her *annus horribilis*, on her forty-fifth wedding anniversary, a substantial part of Windsor Castle burst into flames. Two of her sons, Prince Edward and Prince Andrew, helped to clear the Palace of its art treasures. Her other children got in touch either that day or the next day. The notable absentee on this occasion was her husband, the Duke of Edinburgh, who was in South America and did not fly home until a day or two later, in time for the banquet at which the *annus horribilis* speech was made. It is no secret that the Queen and her husband lead separate lives, and have done for years. To what extent it was an 'arranged' marriage we shall perhaps never fully know, but she had certainly considered him as an eligible partner from her early teens, and there is no evidence that in these early adolescent years she ever seriously considered an alternative partner, though two Dukes were both suggested to her as possibilities.

Partly because the Queen has been held in very great affection by the British people, and partly out of fear, it was only in recent times that anyone would have dreamed of writing openly about such matters. The Queen and Prince Philip often eat their meals apart, and they spend their evenings, if they do not have company, in separate apartments, the Queen watching television or struggling with the *Daily Telegraph* crossword by her electric fire with only her corgis for companionship, the Duke otherwise engaged. To all outward appearances, the Royal pair are represented as ideal figures. To those of a younger generation this would seem like hypocrisy, but the truth is that nearly all systems – political, religious, social – depend to a very large degree on what could be called hypocrisy, or could equally well be called keeping up appearances.

Speculations about the Royal Marriage were frequent in its early days, but there were certain things which were Never Written, though they might have been gossiped about by courtiers and by those who took an interest in such matters.

One example was the supposed mistresses of the Duke of Edinburgh. This was a fact noted by Fiametta Rocco in a major interview with Prince Philip in the British newspaper the *Independent on Sunday*.* With extraordinary candour, Ms Rocco confronted the Duke with the rumours of his infidelities over the years, to receive the reply, 'Have you ever stopped to think that for the last forty years I have never moved anywhere without a policeman accompanying me? So how the *hell* could I get away with anything like that?' There are plenty of answers to that. But the remarkable

*December 13, 1992.

thing about this conversation is not whether you believe Prince Philip's answer; the remarkable thing is that such an exchange should have been happening at all. In the inconceivable event of King George V having granted an 'interview' to a journalist,* you can guess his response if the said journalist had quizzed His Majesty about jaunts to boarding houses in Bognor.

'The papers continually accuse Philip of having been a harsh father,' the Queen Mother once remarked to a dinner-companion. 'If they only knew the truth . . .' her voice trailed away, and she gave a little shrug. 'It was always Lilibet who was too strict, and Philip who tried to moderate her.'† No one outside the immediate family circle could test the truth of this highly subjective judgement. In any event, it would seem to have been easier to be born a daughter than a son of the House of Windsor. Princess Anne shows fewer signs of emotional scarring than her brothers, but this is partly because she has chosen to reveal herself much less to the prurient view of television cameras and newspapers. There also remain the facts of her divorce and her many unhappy dependencies on such figures as Royal bodyguards and policemen. If it is true that children learn how to be married by watching their parents, then the young Windsors will have had some distinctive role models. One cannot fail to admire the pluck and constancy of Prince Philip and the Queen, who undoubtedly have a strong partnership of

* Though George V never gave an interview, it is an interesting historical fact that the first modern royalty to grant an 'interview' to the Press was King George's cousin the Kaiser, while staying at Osborne House on the Isle of Wight after the death of Queen Victoria.
† Private information.

sorts as they begin to face old age; but it is a partnership based on much separation, and it is not what a bourgeois person would recognise as a 'happy' marriage. Certainly the modern idea that married people should contrive to do everything, including sleeping, together has never been part of Prince Philip's or the Queen's idea of how a Royal couple should conduct themselves. They themselves had some distinctive role models to follow. Queen Elizabeth was a notoriously 'devoted' wife to George VI, but his last hours were spent alone, drinking chocolate and smoking a cigarette in bed, and it was left to a servant to find him dead some time the next morning. Philip's parents brought him up in an extraordinary way – with no fixed home. His parents separated when he was young, and by Royal standards there was very little money. His mother, a constant figure in his life (she lived in Buckingham Palace in latter days), was, as we have already mentioned, a nun.

Whatever contemporary psychiatrists might consider the perfect school for 'normal' or 'happy' marriage, this cannot have been it. And if this is the background to the marriages of Prince Charles's parents and grandparents, the emotionally unsatisfactory nature of Lady Diana Spencer's background is equally well known. The beautiful but emotionally brittle Frances Roche 'bolted' after thirteen years of marriage to Johnnie Spencer. No family therapist or marriage guidance counsellor would imagine, when they saw the wedding of Prince Charles and Lady Diana Spencer, that they were going to have an easy time.

The marriage of 'the Waleses' was from the first the subject of stupendous, unimaginably intense observation: 600 million people watched it on television. What would Hitler or Stalin not have done to achieve audiences of this size and scale?

Lady Diana Spencer chose as her wedding-hymn 'I vow to thee, my country', a religious air more associated in England with times of war and periods of national emergency than with nuptial celebration. Until pacifism became the prevailing fad in the Church of England, it was sung annually at Armistice Services. In that hymn she prayed to be inspired with the love that asks no questions, the love which asks no price, but lays upon the altar the final sacrifice; and all this was done in a spirit of simple patriotism. For those watching the solemnities, it gave new meaning to the old phrase about lying back and thinking of England.

Since almost every male in Great Britain had fallen in love with Lady Diana, there was inevitably some ambivalence in the national response to this act of supreme sacrifice. Auberon Waugh had observed, shortly after their engagement, 'We must all decide that 19-year-old Lady Diana Spencer is innocent, truthful, sweet and entirely delicious. What has Wales done to deserve her? More particularly, what has she done to deserve such a hellish fate?'* Few of the professional 'Royal-watchers' understood that this was what she was letting herself in for – a 'hellish fate'. Even so, after her honeymoon, Lady Diana confided to reporters: 'I never thought it was possible to be so happy't, though she did not say whether the cause of her happiness was what had happened during the previous two weeks, or the fact that the honeymoon was now over.

Certainly, to all outward appearances, it seemed as though Lady Diana, in the first years of marriage, was defying her grandmother Lady Fermoy's advice and submitting with great fortitude to the final sacrifice. Rumours

Private Eye, November 29, 1980.
†Elizabeth Longford, *The Royal House of Windsor* (1984 revised edition) p.281.

1a Queen Victoria, Prince Albert and their children at Osborne, Isle of Wight. Prince Albert left his descendents the difficult legacy of being an 'ideal family'.

1b Queen Victoria with 'Bertie' and his Danish wife Princess Alexandra. Bertie's repeated adulteries provided the public with entertainment and did much to revive the popularity of the Monarchy which had plummeted during Queen Victoria's widowhood.

2a Queen Mary visits a Welsh coal-mine.
Her bolt-upright posture seldom varied.

2b George V making the first Royal Christmas broadcast in 1934.

3a The former King, Edward VIII, commits the crime of marrying for love, 3 June 1937. At the new Queen's insistence, Duchess Wallis was never allowed to be Her Royal Highness.

3b How the news of the Abdication reached the streets of London.

4a The new Queen's 'homely' appearance helped to create her 'virtuous' image with the public. Here she is pictured with her daughters, the future Queen Elizabeth II, and Princess Margaret Rose.

4b 'Now we can look the East End in the face.' The King and Queen, when their own palace had been hit by enemy bombs, built up a particular rapport with bomb victims.

5 Sir James Gunn's 'Conversation Piece at Royal Lodge, Windsor, 1950', is one of the most successful pieces of royal iconography. The Queen holds the teapot ('Who'll be mother?') as the princesses lean forward, perhaps wondering whether their father will speak. A corgi snoozes beneath his chair.

6a Princess Elizabeth makes a 21st birthday speech to the Empire – significantly, it is made in Cape Town, South Africa, 22 April 1947.

6b Prince Philip, the handsome Duke of Edinburgh, was a serving officer in the Royal Navy until his wife became the Queen.

7a The coronation of Queen Elizabeth II in Westminster Abbey.

7b Coronation photograph of Queen Elizabeth II and Philip, Duke of Edinburgh.

8 The Queen's devotion to her father's Empire, now re-named the British Commonwealth, never diminishes. This photograph shows Her Majesty's visit to the spice island of Grenada, 13 February 1966.

9a Not everyone would consider the influence of 'Uncle Dickie' (Lord Mountbatten of Burma) to have been a happy one. He tried to persuade the Queen to change the name of her family to Mountbatten Windsor — a proposal which led to a major rift between the Queen and Mountbatten's nephew Philip.

9b Corgis and the indomitable mother have been a constant feature of the Queen's grown-up life.

9c Sisters. The Queen's unchanging gum boots and headscarf never looked fashionable and therefore never dated. Princess Margaret's modish outfit, worn at Badminton 1971, already looks like an exhibit in a museum of costume.

9d The familiar sight of the Queen Trooping the Colour is one which most British people would miss if the Monarchy were modernized or abolished.

10a Prince Charles being welcomed to Trinity College, Cambridge (where he studied for three years) by the Master, Lord Butler.

10b Charles at his Investiture in Caernarvon, North Wales, 1 July 1969. This ancient ceremony was invented by David Lloyd George to gratify his Welsh constituents and was first enacted by the future Edward VIII.

11a Prince Andrew on his twenty-first birthday. He later went on to serve as a Royal Navy helicopter pilot in Margaret Thatcher's war against the Argentine.

11b Margaret Thatcher's known hostility to the British Commonwealth was one of the many areas where she differed from her sovereign.

12a Happy in love – the famous engagement photograph taken at Buckingham Palace, 24 February 1981.

12b The Royal pair on one of their first visits abroad together – here pictured in Bunbury, near Perth, Western Australia.

13 Before long Lady Diana Spencer had flowered into the Fairy Princess – a figure who was poised to do more damage to the British Monarchy than anyone since Oliver Cromwell.

14a Skiing in Klosters. At first Lady Di and the Duchess of York were friends, but they soon became rivals for public attention.

14b Meanwhile, the Prince of Wales continued to see his friend Mrs Parker-Bowles, seen here after a polo match.

15a Fire at Windsor Castle nearly destroys the Queen's childhood home.

15b Her Majesty delivers her famous 'annus horribilis' speech at the Mansion House, November 1992.

16 The Princess of Wales, on holiday in Austria
with Prince William and Prince Harry, April 1993.

that all was not well with the marriage in those early years, when she had slept with her husband with at least enough frequency to produce a couple of fine sons, only added to the general feeling that she was doing a good job, as she accompanied her husband on his tours of duty and, with increasing frequency, appeared as a patroness in her 'own right' of various charitable, cultural or public concerns. True, it was less than eighteen months after Lady Diana's marriage that, in December 1982, in his column in the *Daily Mail*, Dempster revealed that Lady Diana was 'a very wilful and spoiled girl. Suddenly, getting this enormous power, having people curtsy and bow to her, doing everything she wants, she's become a fiend. She has become a little monster.'

Ten years later, the Princess's biographer, Andrew Morton, revealed that this criticism had caused Lady Diana particular pain. Morton's version of what had happened to her since she married makes compulsive reading. While she suffered from post-natal depression as a result of Prince William's birth (June 21, 1982), Lady Diana had not been cheered up by the continuing closeness of her husband's relationship with Mrs Parker-Bowles. After the birth of his son, the Prince was frequently away from home. 'Whatever happens, I will always love you,' he said on one of the evenings he happened to be at Kensington Palace. But his wife did not find the words particularly reassuring; they were said into a portable telephone (presumably to Mrs Parker-Bowles, perhaps to one of his other attachments), while his wife whimpered and eavesdropped in an adjoining room.

Not only was he, as we now learn, entirely unsympathetic to his wife's eating disorder, bulimia nervosa, but he was also dismayed by her extremely modern, not to say middle-class, attitude to the marriage conventions. 'During a ferocious argument with Diana, Charles made clear the Royal Family's position. He told her in no uncertain terms that his father, the Duke of Edinburgh, had agreed that if, after five years, his marriage was not working he could go back to his bachelor habits. Whether those sentiments, uttered in the heat of the moment, are true or not was beside the point,' adds Andrew Morton. 'They had the effect of placing Diana on her guard in her every dealing with her in-laws.'

Some of Mr Morton's readers might decide that it matters very much indeed whether these words 'were true or not' – first, whether they were uttered, and second, whether they represent the Royal Family's attitude to marriage.

One's answer to the first question must depend upon a whole bundle of irrational things, which include how one feels about Lady Diana herself. ('Diana Spencer,' said the vicar's wife in Norfolk all those years ago, 'if you tell one more lie like that I am going to make you walk home.')* Those with an experience of giving, or receiving, confidences about marital feuds will know how much 'editing' takes place, often quite unconsciously, on the teller's part.

Certainly, as a supposed statement by Prince Charles, it is extremely odd – so odd, some would say, that it would have been difficult to invent. Some would think it odd to consult one's father about the permissibility or otherwise of committing adultery, but we now all know enough about Prince Charles to know that he is an extremely odd man. Historians cannot at this juncture pronounce with any certainty whether he said it or not, and whether or not Prince Philip introduced a 'five-year rule', whereby the Prince of Wales had to endure a further three years after making the alleged statement before feeling able to philander with a free

*Morton, op. cit. p.21.

conscience. But whether or not these exact words were said at this exact juncture, the general view expressed of the married state is surely one which has operated in the House of Windsor throughout its history.

What has contributed in such large measure to the difficulties of the Royal Family in the present generation is that the wives of the two Princes – Lady Diana Spencer and Sarah Ferguson – expected their husbands to behave like modern middle-class husbands rather than Edwardian aristocrats.

One of King Edward VII's most devoted mistresses – so close to him that Queen Alexandra invited her to attend the King's deathbed – was Mrs Alice Keppel. Some sixty years after Mrs Keppel took her touching farewell of her Sovereign and lover, her great-great-granddaughter, Camilla, met the great-great-grandson of Edward VII. Having informed Prince Charles of the tenuous ancestral connection between them, Camilla is supposed to have said, 'How about it then?' – the beginning of a fond attachment.

It would be quite wrong to suppose that Victorian and Edwardian upper-class marriages, with their high incidence of 'contained' adultery, caused no pain. The biographers of Edward VII and of Queen Alexandra do not tell a story of smiling indulgence on the wife's side, nor of guilt-free sensuality on the husband's. Even *The Times* said in 1890 that it would be 'affectation to conceal' the reason why such huge crowds had attended a production of *She Stoops to Conquer* at the Haymarket Theatre. It was because the Prince of Wales insisted on bringing his wife to see his mistress perform in the part of Kate Hardcastle. In 1891, for example, we read of poor 'Alix', unable to bear the humiliation of the very public knowledge of her husband's adultery with Lady Brooke – known because of her indiscretions as

The Babbling Brooke. In consequence she refused to attend his fiftieth birthday party, and went off to the Crimea with her sister, the Empress of Russia. All this seemed like a mirror of what was going on in Kensington Palace in 1992.

Yet those who have studied the period, or those old and grand enough to recall it, have assured us that Edwardian marriages survived because of the existence of a code. The observance of this code meant that, on the surface of things at least, the institutions and great houses which these marriages cemented were unthreatened by the frailty of those who were born to uphold them. Divorce took place – inevitably – among the upper classes in early-twentieth-century England; but the vigorous families, and the ones which survived most triumphantly as political powers, were not necessarily those where no infidelity was known, but where wives and husbands were tolerant and prepared to 'weather the storm'.

Diana belonged to a generation where you hoped to marry for 'love'. When 'love' dies or fades, or changes into something else, you consult a therapist – either a psychotherapist, a sex therapist or some other kind of therapist. If that fails, and you are both sufficiently young and vigorous, or sufficiently optimistic, to suppose that happiness might be found with a different partner, you decide that the marriage is over and you file for a 'civilised' divorce, trying to hide from yourself the devastating effect this is having on your children. Such is modern marriage, European- and American-style. One of the strange facts about modern life, in spite of its supposedly more relaxed attitude to sexual morality, is that adultery *per se* should be seen as grounds for a divorce. The 'old' view of marriage is perfectly encapsulated in an exchange between the great eighteenth-century moralist Dr Samuel Johnson and his biographer James Boswell: 'I mentioned to him a dispute between a friend of mine [in fact Boswell himself] and his lady, concerning conjugal infidelity, which my friend had maintained was by no means so bad in the husband, as in the wife. *Johnson*: 'Your friend was in the right, Sir. Between a man and his Maker it is a different question: but between a man and his wife, a husband's infidelity is nothing. They are connected by children, by fortune, by serious considerations of community. Wise married women don't trouble themselves about infidelity in their husbands . . .'

Unappealing as this might be to modern feminist sensibilities, it is hard to see how a Royal Family (or, come to that, an American Presidential family) could be sustained unless it took this attitude. Added to the naturally conservative approach to divorce which any person might wish to share, the Royal Family are obliged to embody in their own weak persons an office of State. It was with irony, but truth, that George VI and Queen Elizabeth spoke of their little family unit – themselves and the two princesses – as 'The Firm'. Those who have since married into 'The Firm' have, as the Queen and her subjects might have hoped, undertaken to promote the values and purposes of 'The Firm'. Without such intentions on both sides, irreparable damage was bound to be done to the young people involved, to their marriages and to 'The Firm' itself.

Had the present Queen been a character built in the Edward VII mould, it might have been much easier for anyone wishing to marry her children to be cynical and to realise what they were letting themselves in for. As it happens, she was the child of George VI and Elizabeth Bowes-Lyon, a couple who did not always observe the borderline which exists between a seemly desire to keep up appearances and a crippling hypocrisy.

*

One of the most potent images which they wished to present of themselves was enshrined by Sir James Gunn in his beautiful group portrait of the King, the Queen and the two Princesses at Royal Lodge. It greets any visitor to the National Portrait Gallery in London, and it is one of the most potent visual declarations of what the New Monarchy (by contrast with Edward VIII) so firmly stood for. Nothing could more confidently and primly have proclaimed the difference between Elizabeth Bowes-Lyon, her reassuring plumpness, her sweet smile, her dear young daughters, her hand stretched out to be 'mother' with the teapot – and the exiled Duchess of Windsor, fast, worldly, beautiful, childless, thin, jewel-bedecked. In spite of the beautiful Gothick interior in which they sit, there is something essentially middle-class about this icon. They are the perfect mid-twentieth-century, classless nuclear family, who have struggled through the Second World War with their ration books and their austere simple tastes, and will continue through the peace to be emblems of happy family virtue.

Since the despised David, the Duke of Windsor, and Wallis had been honest enough, selfish and naïve enough, to marry for love, whatever it cost them, Queen Elizabeth (later the Queen Mother) never lost the opportunity to emphasise to the public that the new proprietors of 'The Firm' stood firm for Family Values. The last thing any of those four round the table would ever contemplate would be a horrible divorce, such as That Wallis Woman had allowed herself – not once, but twice.

If that is the message of James Gunn's picture, and of thousands of comparable royal icons put out during the 1940s and 1950s, we can now see that the King and

Queen were piling up trouble for the future. One figure in that group of four – Princess Margaret – fell in love with one of her father's equerries, Group-Captain Peter Townsend, who was divorced from his wife in 1952. It was of course unthinkable, only twenty years after her mother had become Queen of England on the 'No divorce please, we're Royal' ticket, that Princess Margaret should have married this man. The King was told that, if they married in such circumstances, Princess Margaret would not be eligible for a Civil List pension. Since the King was only worth several million pounds, it would obviously have been beyond his own capacities to provide his daughter with any such allowance. Group Captain Townsend has subsequently, a little ungallantly, told friends that he might have married the Princess in defiance of the conventions had they had enough money to live on. These pecuniary considerations were swept to one side, however, when – with what some of their friends considered nauseating humbug – a statement was issued to the Press indicating that 'I would like it to be known that I have decided not to marry Group Captain Peter Townsend. I have been aware that, subject to my renouncing my rights of succession, it might have been possible for me to contract a civil marriage. But, mindful of the Church's teaching that Christian marriage is indissoluble, and conscious of my duty to the Commonwealth, I have resolved to put these considerations before any others.' Conscious of her duty to the Commonwealth, the Princess then married a charming photographer called Tony Armstrong-Jones. The marriage ended in 1976. (Decree absolute 1978.)

The other young figure in James Gunn's icon, the future Queen Elizabeth II, has not, at the time of writing, sought a divorce, but it is noticeable that, out of her four children, three have been married and three have had marriages which came unstuck. In other words, from that first ideal 'nuclear family' of George VI and Elizabeth Bowes-Lyon, which was supposed to be so much more reassuring than the (in fact devotedly happily married) Wallis and David Windsor, not one marriage has survived. It seems that the Queen's is a polite shell of which it has only recently been possible for people to speak. Princess Margaret's ended; Prince Charles's has ended, Prince Andrew's has ended and Princess Anne has lately demonstrated the triumph of hope over experience by divorcing one nonentity and marrying another. One does not need to parody Lady Bracknell by saying that to have had one unhappy marriage in the family may be deemed a misfortune, but to have had five begins to look like carelessness.

What Lady Fermoy, in her delicate warning to Lady Diana, should have said was: 'It is not difficult to be married to any member of this family. It is impossible.'

Lady Fermoy was in a better position than most of us to recognise that British Royal personages are actually different from the rest of mankind, different even from the rich and the aristocratic who live in comparably large houses and employ a comparable number of servants. Being Royal is itself a kind of selfishness. It would take a saint born into the Royal Family to draw a border between respect which was owing to the Crown and slavishness owing to their Royal personages. Anyone who has ever had to do with the Royal Family has their own tale to tell of capriciousness which in a private individual would be insupportable. King George VI, for example, like his daughter after him, seldom found himself sitting at the same dinner-table as his wife. He was often left alone in the evenings, and he did not like it. In consequence, he would habitually telephone an equerry and demand his presence. Group Captain Townsend was not the only Royal equerry at this period whose marriage ended in divorce. Single people are better equipped than the married to be Royal servants.

There is of course a distinction between being a Royal servant and being a Royal friend, but it is not always one which the Windsors know how to observe. Princess Margaret's friends are devoted to her, but one seldom meets any of them, after they have had the Princess to stay, without hearing a tale of woe – how she has kept the company up until four in the morning (it is supposedly not allowed to withdraw from a room until a Royal personage has done so); or insisted on winning at parlour games, even those such as Trivial Pursuit which require a degree of knowledge which she simply did not possess; how she has expected her hostess to act as a lady-in-waiting, drawing back the curtains in the morning, and so forth.

Prince Charles is no less lordly in his own way, and his brother Prince Andrew, a rather sadly friendless figure, thought nothing in his bachelor days of commanding the presence of young people whom he barely knew at Buckingham Palace to make up parties. This is the sort of behaviour which all four children of the Queen grew up as believing to be normal. Their parents might have been 'severe' with them, but no one in the family questioned their inherent superiority to the rest of mankind, an idea which was inextricably tied up with reverence for the Crown itself. 'From his childhood onwards,' said Keir Hardie about the birth of the future Edward VIII in 1894, 'this boy will be surrounded by sycophants and flatterers by the score.' Nothing much has changed since 1894 – except the world, a fact which the House of Windsor has been slow to notice. A friend of mine had grown-up children who objected to lining up and bowing, morning and evening, when they had a member of the Royal Family to stay in their house. They were wrong to object, said this loyal hostess: if you have a Royal Family you have to retain the idea that the Crown is to be reverenced, and you have to try to befriend the person trapped inside the royal carapace; 'because', said this kind lady, 'they need friends'.

Like Richard II in Shakespeare's play, the Windsors live with bread, feel want, taste grief and need friends. This does not mean that it is particularly easy to be their friend, and if ordinary friendship is seen to be impossible one begins to see why marriage in these circumstances is next to impossible. Those on the outer reaches of the Royal Family – such as the Kents, both the Duke of Kent and his brother Prince Michael, or the Duke of Gloucester – have managed to combine a life of public service with a relatively 'normal' way of life. Their spouses have obviously had strains which are not placed on the shoulders of wholly non-Royal personages,* but by and large they are able to lead private lives. Their marriages and their careers or their functions in life have been somehow distinct. But for those who have married the Queen's children or her sister, this has not been the case. In taking on their marriage partner they have also taken on that partner's career. Marriage has almost been a 'job' for them – a job from which there has been no vacation.

The role-model for this 'job' has been the Duke of Edinburgh. All his biographers, and all the perceptive journalists who have ever studied Prince Philip, have noticed that he had a very hard time as a young man adjusting to his marital status, particularly after his wife

---

*The strains include persistent and open malice from the 'hard core' Royals such as the Queen Mother, who never misses an opportunity to denigrate Princess Michael, the Duchess of Kent, et al.

became the Queen of England. Michael Parker, Prince Philip's former Secretary, has said, 'He told me the first day he offered me my job that *his* job, first, second and last, was never to let her down.' He has fairly heroically fulfilled this function – and one says that knowing full well that he has always been as discreet and as publicly loyal as any human being could have been. No one could expect in their youth that their actions might one day be subject to the searchlight of Kitty Kelley's investigative glare; and no human life would survive such scrutiny. Having your life written by Kitty Kelley is like appearing before the judgement seat of an unmerciful Deity; most of us are able to live in this world without such exposure, knowing that it would only be in the world to come, if at all, that 'the secrets of all hearts shall be revealed'. Nevertheless, the burdens of being a Royal spouse have been visible in Prince Philip's manner and demeanour ever since his father-in-law the King died prematurely of lung cancer. Someone who was present in Kenya when the news of the King's death came remarked, 'I remember seeing her moments after she became Queen – moments, not hours – and she seemed almost to reach out for it. There were no tears. She was just there, back braced, her colour a little heightened. Just waiting for her destiny. It was quite different for Philip. He sat slumped behind a copy of *The Times*. He didn't want it at all. It was going to change his whole life: take away the emotional stability he'd finally found.' Another person who watched the Royal couple at this time said, 'I'll never forget it. He looked as if half the world had fallen on him.'*

The first thing to happen to Philip was that he lost his naval career. He was perhaps not the most brilliant officer who had ever served in the Royal Navy, but he

---

*Quoted by Fiametta Rocco, *Independent on Sunday* December 13, 1992.

was perfectly adequate and a good deal better liked than his popinjay uncle, Lord Mountbatten, had been when he was in the Senior Service. Speaking forty years later to a journalist, Prince Philip said, '"It wasn't my ambition to be president of the Mint Advisory Committee. I didn't want to be president of the World Wildlife Fund. I was asked to do it" – he says, staring out of the Palace windows, his face set. "I'd have much rather stayed in the Navy, frankly."'*

It was shortly after the Coronation that Philip, who felt his very identity was being eroded by the experience of being the faithful Royal spouse, attempted to persuade the Queen to take his surname. There was some pathos in this, since it was only a surname which he had adopted on his marriage. His father's name – if it makes sense to speak of royalties possessing surnames – was Schleswig-Holstein-Sonderburg-Glucksburg. When he married, Philip chose to take the name Mountbatten, the name adopted by his grandfather Prince Louis of Battenberg in 1917 when the Royal House of Saxe-Coburg became the House of Windsor.

To the idea of calling her children 'Mountbatten', the Queen was most adamantly opposed. It had been a feature of Lord Mountbatten's insane ambition and desire to stamp his ego on everything he touched that, as well as persuading the gullible young Philip to adopt his name, he should impose it upon the entire future dynasty of the Royal House. The compromise was suggested that the Queen's children should bear the surname 'Mountbatten-Windsor'. Churchill, the Prime Minister, urged the Queen to stand firm and to call them merely 'Windsor'. At this point Philip exploded with wrath and walked out of the room shouting, 'I'm just a bloody amoeba! That's all!' A secretary who was present at the time says, 'I've always taken it to mean that

*Ibid.

he was just there to deposit semen.'*

It was following this row that an estrangement came – years in which the Queen and Prince Philip were only notionally and publicly 'together'. Prince Philip usually travelled abroad on his own. All this was handled with the utmost discretion, and it is only right to say courage, by Prince Philip, and probably by the Queen herself. But it would be foolish to pretend that this heroic charade – the marriage of Queen Elizabeth II and Prince Philip – provided an ideal role model for their children to follow, and it would be equally foolish to believe that anyone other than Prince Philip would be able to stay the course.

The pressure on Royal spouses is made so much worse by the notion that they should be 'ideal'. And yet, considering the way in which George VI and his Queen came to the throne, it was not entirely unreasonable of them to stress this aspect of Monarchy as so important. No one chose George VI as King because he was cleverer than his brother, or more handsome or more dynamic. In dismissing Edward VIII the Establishment had made it abundantly clear that the King was totally powerless politically, and that the idea of him actually exercising any of his Royal prerogative was laughable. (George VI did indeed try to do so when Churchill became Prime Minister. He objected to Beaverbrook becoming a member of the Cabinet. Relations between George VI and Churchill had been strained since 1936, when Churchill was the most eloquent supporter of the King's Party and Beaverbrook its most energetic propagandist. When George VI made his objections, Churchill ignored them, and when the King summoned Churchill to the Palace to explain himself, this command too was ignored. Not for nothing did Churchill

*Rocco; *Independent on Sunday* December 13, 1992.

choose 'The Battle Hymn of the Republic' as one of his funeral hymns.) Given then the neutered position of the Monarchy after 1936, what else could it be except a religious and moral figurehead to the nation? And, since the notional reason for sending his brother into exile had been a dispute about the doctrine of marriage, the least George VI could bequeath to his heirs was the wholly new and disastrous concept that Royal marriages should be perfect.

In the course of 1992, it became clear how extremely unhappy the marriages of the Queen's children had been. Unhappiness is impossible to quantify. There is no reason to suppose that Charles and Diana, Anne and Mark, or Fergie and Andrew, were any more or less unhappy than their parents. For Elizabeth II, the concept of divorce has not, to date, been a possibility. Her father became King with the words of Archbishop Cosmo Gordon Lang ringing in his ears: 'From God he [Edward VIII] had received a high and sacred trust. Yet by his own will he has abdicated – he has surrendered the trust. With characteristic frankness he has told us his motive. It was a craving for private happiness. Strange and sad it must be that for such a motive, however strongly it pressed upon his heart, he should have disappointed hopes so high and abandoned a trust so great.'

This broadcast – one is tempted to write broadside – by Archbishop Lang was given to speed the departing Edward VIII on his way in 1936, and it was universally condemned at the time as the unjust sport of 'kicking a man when he is down'. ('What is the point in kicking a man,' Lang is alleged to have replied, '*unless* he is down?') It was strange in 1992 to find that some of the stuffier English papers revived the sermon and preached it to the 'younger Royals' – in particular to the Princess of Wales. This was what appeared to give the publication of Andrew Morton's book its significance in the six months or so after its publication. It was one thing for the

Royal couple to be unhappy, and for everyone to infer, from their appearances and non-appearances together in public, that they were unhappy. It was another altogether for their 'craving for private happiness' to threaten the very foundations of the Monarchy itself. For so long as the marital troubles of the Queen's children were merely matters of rumour – even though the whole country might be teeming with such rumours – there was no danger to the Crown. As soon as they openly decided to bring their marriages to an end, the situation radically changed. Since Charles's great-uncle had actually been sent on his way because of the Church's teachings on marriage, how could Charles ever hope to become King? Who could look to Charles as a model of domestic virtue as they had looked to King George VI, and to Elizabeth II in the first forty years of her reign?

If the House of Windsor is to owe its future survival to its record of marital happiness, then it is almost certainly doomed. Its more optimistic supporters have put forward the enterprising notion that this family should not be ideal, it should be representative. This has even led to enthusiastic speculation among the gay lobby about Prince Edward's reasons for choosing a career in the theatre and delaying the announcement of his own wedding.

Whatever the truth of Royal fairy stories, it is unlikely that homosexual propaganda will ever succeed to the point where homosexuality in a Royal man is considered positively desirable. This is probably a mistake. With a plethora of heirs from the minor royalties, and the built-in difficulties which any of the Windsors and their partners were bound to meet in marriage, it might have been better for all concerned if none of the Queen's children had been allowed to marry.

For in the end, the strain of being married to a royal personage was too much – for Anthony Armstrong-Jones; for Diana Spencer; for Mark Phillips, and for Sarah Ferguson. Whatever the individual reasons for the collapse of these marriages, the collective effect of these four failures has been devastating. No doubt Monarchy is one of those things which is best not examined in too strictly utilitarian a manner. If the attempt is made too rigidly to define its functions, these very functions begin to seem insubstantial. Monarchy is really one of those areas of life which justifies the saying that 'the heart has its reasons . . .'

This has not prevented defenders of the Monarchy advancing the view that the domestic virtue of the Royal Family was an essential part of the Crown's role in national life. Had the Bourbons or the Borgias or the Hapsburgs taken this line, many of the greatest Monarchs in European history would have been forced to resign their thrones. Frederick the Great, arguably the most distinguished Monarch of the eighteenth century, would hardly have passed the Bowes-Lyon 'respectability' test, and even Lady Di might have been forgiven for wondering whether he was heterosexual.

In the past it was one of the prerogatives of royal personages that they could behave more sinfully than their subjects. In twentieth-century Britain they are for some reason expected to be more virtuous. In his very Abdication speech, Edward VIII had contrasted himself with his good, monogamous brother, the Duke of York: 'He has one matchless blessing, enjoyed by so many of you, but not by me – a happy home with his wife and children.' The 'happy home' image was exploited for rather more than it was worth by King George VI's Queen, and it was something which their daughter, Elizabeth II, was prepared to go along with – though one suspects that among the things which made her 'happy' marriage and motherhood probably came rather low down on the list of preferences. (Grandmotherhood is evidently a different matter, but she never gave the impression of liking any of her children except Andrew more than she liked horses and dogs.)

At the time of the Silver Jubilee, the Queen made a speech at the Guildhall. 'I think everyone will concede that today, of all occasions, I should begin my speech with "My husband and I".' This was not a bad joke – her habitual use of the cliché in broadcasts and speeches had been lampooned for so long. Then, with one of those leaden pleasantries which are presumably believed by royal speech writers to 'lighten' the tone, she quoted the bishop who, when asked for his opinion of sin, replied, 'I am against it.' The Queen went on to say that if asked her opinion of family life, she would say, simply, 'I am for it.'

Clearly none of her immediate in-laws was able to echo her. Whatever else the British Monarchy will be in the coming decades, it will hardly be able to represent itself as an emblem of happy, unified, Christian family life. Of course, there was never any reason why it should. Some of the most impressive Monarchs in British history have either been unmarried, like Queen Elizabeth I, or figures who scarcely represent 'family values' at their best. (One thinks of Charles II or George IV.) The self-righteous way in which the House of Windsor advertised themselves as the ultimate Happy Family was their excuse not merely for exiling King Edward VIII, but also for refusing so much as to be on terms with his wife. The feud which the Queen Mother kept up with the Duchess of Windsor for over forty years was no doubt conducted with the highest of Christian motives. The monogamous principle could not have been more fiercely underlined than in Queen Elizabeth's insistence that her sister-in-law must be denied even the title of Her Royal Highness.

Not long ago, in defiance of the laws of trespass, I stood beside the Duchess's modest little grave at Frogmore, in the shadow of the enormous mausoleum built by Queen Victoria to the memory of her sainted husband Prince Albert. When I thought of the emaciated body which they had lowered into that grave with such maimed rites, I momentarily hoped that the dead can witness our doings here; for in the 'scandals' of Fergie, Di, Mark Phillips and Princess Margaret, Wallis surely would have read the visitation of Nemesis.

EIGHT

The House of Windsor
and the Church

The King's Majesty hath the chief power in this
Realm of England, and other of his Dominions,
unto whom the chief Government of all Estates
in this Realm, whether they be Ecclesiastical or
Civil, in all causes doth appertain . . . The Bishop
of Rome hath no jurisdiction in this realm of
England.

Articles of Religion, Book of Common Prayer

On one of the few occasions when I met Princess Margaret,
the Queen's sister, I was arrested by the seriousness with
which she took the Queen's religious role. 'She is God's
representative in this realm,' the Princess said to me,
in language which might have made very good sense if
spoken about an English Queen in 1588 or even, if you had
a sympathetic audience, in 1888, but which sounded odd
in 1988. Why should it have sounded odd? Not because
the Queen is anything but a good Christian woman. In a
nebulous, indefinable sense, one feels not merely that she
exercises a religious function, but that this could perhaps
be seen as the most important part of her role. But when we
come to examine the legal and practical implications of the
Queen's religious role, you realise that she is locked into a
number of very deep difficulties. These are not difficulties
of her making; perhaps they were always inherent in the
Erastian idea (the control of religion by the State), but they

have greatly increased because of the changes which have happened in England since she was a young woman. And this has less to do, strangely enough, with the secularisation of British society than with the growth of religions other than the Queen's.

If all the non-Anglicans in the United Kingdom were agnostics or atheists, the ceremonies of the Coronation and the orotund phrases of the Prayer Book concerning the Queen's Most Excellent Majesty would probably be lovingly preserved. But it is difficult to maintain a religious establishment in a country where most religious people do not share the religion of the Monarch. England today – with its abundance of devout Moslems, Roman Catholics, Hindus, Sikhs, Mormons – is not the England of which Elizabeth II was crowned Queen in 1953. The attempt to maintain a religious establishment in a country where more people than not have a religion different from that of the Queen does not work; and anyone who doubts that should read the history of nineteenth-century Ireland. But if the Establishment is broken, does that not mean that one of the most important functions of the Queen has been abandoned and that one of the most potent reasons for maintaining a Monarchy has been dissolved?

The Crown has a religious, as well as a political, significance in British history. It might be truer to say it has a religious function. It is not merely a nebulous 'spiritual' function, teaching us that all power is ultimately from above* (though monarchists might derive comfort from such thoughts). Part of the actual, and practical, role of the King or Queen is to be the Supreme Governor of the Church of England. All bishops of the Church of England and the deans of the Cathedrals are technically speaking appointed by the Crown. So, too, are the Regius Professors of Divinity at the older universities, and the Prebendaries and Canonries of the various 'Royal Peculiars'. It is, of course, the Prime Minister's task to find suitable candidates for vacant bishoprics – hence Lord Melbourne's famous 'Damn it, another bishop is dead', and Lord Salisbury's 'I believe they die to spite me'. Although in practice neither the Monarch nor the Prime Minister alone is responsible for selecting all these clergymen today (they are chosen by the Prime Minister's Patronage Secretary in consultation with various ecclesiastical advisers), every one of them, before accepting his office in the Church of God, has to take an oath of secular allegiance to the Crown. This quite inevitably means that only believers in, or tolerators of, the idea of Religious Establishment can serve the Church of England in this way. Those who believe in the principle of 'Render to Caesar the things that are Caesar's and unto God the things that are God's' are obliged either to stay out of the Established Church or to take their Erastian vows to the Monarch in bad faith.

For many historical reasons, the Church of England has grown unhappy with its position as the Established Religion, and most members of it would not wish the Establishment to continue. This has less to do with the role of the Monarch in ecclesiastical life and more to do with the possibility of the secular Parliament having control over ecclesiastical affairs. The Anglican folk-memory of 1928 is

---

*Vide the Book of Common Prayer: 'ALMIGHTY God, Whose kingdom is everlasting, and power infinite; Have mercy upon the whole Church; and so rule the heart of Thy chosen servant ELIZABETH our Queen and Governor, that she (knowing whose minister she is) may above all things seek Thy honour and glory: and that we, and all her subjects (duly considering whose authority she hath), may faithfully serve, honour and humbly obey her . . .'

bitter: that was the year in which the Church's attempt to revise its own liturgy was prevented by the alliance of Protestants and Anglo-Catholics in the Church with Members of Parliament; and a House of Commons substantially composed of Jews, Agnostics, Roman Catholics and other Nonconformists refused to make legal the Revised Prayer Book. Such a débâcle is unlikely to repeat itself – especially since the Church of England has its own General Synod in which it can debate and to a large extent decide its own destiny. But for any major change in its laws – for example, in its decision to ordain women to the priesthood – it is still beholden to the secular Parliament at Westminster. Women cannot become priests in England until the matter is ratified by Parliament and by the Monarch. Predictably, those opposed to women's ordination hoped to use the Royal Prerogative as a means of blocking the legislation, even after it passed the General Synod, and even if it were approved by Parliament. 'MY SISTER WOULD NEVER ALLOW WOMEN PRIESTS', said one hopeful headline, purporting (rather plausibly, I thought) to quote the words of Princess Margaret.

As it happens, Queen Elizabeth II is a very devout Christian and a believer in the Establishment of the National Church. The great majority of practising worshippers in the Church of England feel a personal affection for her, quite regardless of what they might believe concerning 'Establishment' or the question of 'whose authority she hath'. But the feelings of unease expressed by senior churchmen and ordinary churchgoers about the future cannot be ignored. What would happen if they were to have a Monarch who was not in good faith with the Church? For example, what would happen – which looks all too likely – if Prince Charles were to be divorced? The Church of England forbids the remarriage of divorced persons. This would surely put the Church and the Crown in an impossible position if a divorced King were to inherit his mother's throne.

This is a real conundrum, and it could certainly put paid to Prince Charles's chance of inheriting the throne, just as his great-uncle's wish to marry a divorced woman in 1936 cost him the throne. The situation in 1936, however, was very different from the situation today. Prince Charles's dilemma only serves to highlight the much more drastic division between the Monarch's defined role in law and the actual reality of the situation in Britain today. It is the widening gap between the Sovereign's idea of herself and the reality of things which poses the crisis here. How can the Queen continue to be the Supreme Governor of a Church which, in general, does not wish to continue the Establishment? And even if it did, how could such an Establishment be continued, with its bishops in the House of Lords, and its claims – for example in the language of the Coronation Service – that the Queen is the religious representative of her people, when so few of her subjects share her religious beliefs?

Fidei Defensor, Defender of the Faith, is one of the British Monarch's oldest titles. It was granted to Henry VIII by the Pope for writing a tract on the Seven Sacraments, and for denouncing Luther. The 'Faith' in this august title is the Catholic and Roman Faith. Thereafter, Henry VIII declared himself to be the Supreme Governor of the Church *in* England, and during the reign of Elizabeth I, his daughter, the Church *of* England was brought into being as part of the so-called Elizabethan Settlement.

After the Revolution of 1688, the ruling class were determined that there should be no repetition of the James II fiasco. Since James was a Catholic convert and his particular offences had taken a very Catholic form – in the matter of suppressing the Heads of Houses at Oxford and putting the Seven Bishops on trial – a new doctrine was invented: that the British Monarch might neither be, nor marry, a Catholic. This rule applies not merely to those in the likely running for the Crown, but to any of the Sovereign's heirs. Prince Michael of Kent (fourteenth in line to the throne) in our own day had to seek the Queen's permission before marrying his Catholic spouse; he also had to renounce any claim to the throne.

The days have long since passed when British Catholics felt a conflict of loyalty between their allegiance to the Pope and their allegiance to the Crown. Guy Fawkes, who attempted to blow up the King and Parliament with gunpowder and to place the Catholic Lady Arabella Stuart on the English throne, has been dead for nearly 400 years. The idea that Catholicism might pose a threat to the State was abandoned by the Houses of Parliament in 1829, when they passed the Catholic Emancipation Act, allowing Catholics to attend Universities and Inns of Court, to enter the professions, and to stand for Parliament. Only the Monarch and her family are still stuck in penal times over this question.

As a young man, Prince Charles used to take this extremely seriously, and there were a number of likely brides, of a variety of nationalities, who had to be rejected on the grounds that he would one day be the Supreme Governor of the Church of England. As Supreme Governor, he would be legally entitled to marry a Hindu, a Quaker, an Atheist, a Parsee. The one category of being whom he could never marry would be someone who remained loyal to that Faith of which he was supposed to be the Defender. This ruled out the daughter of the Duke of Wellington – Lady Jane Wellesley – who was dabbling with Catholicism at the time when the Prince was dabbling with her, as well as such Continental princesses and eligible brides as the Princesses of Liechtenstein.

The Queen's position as Supreme Governor of the Church of England is comparable to her position as Head of the Commonwealth. That is to say, an impartial observer could be forgiven for thinking that she was presiding over something which in most palpable terms had ceased to exist. The Church of England, almost by definition, is, or was, a National Church, one of the most distinctive features of Renaissance nationalism. We can now see, from a perspective of 400 years, that the evolution or creation of the Church of England was all of a piece with England's development as a highly independent, belligerent island nation. It is no accident that it evolved in the century in which English sea-power established supremacy even over the mighty maritime empire of Spain, and in which Shakespeare showed himself the Lord of Language.

Plenty of potentates have quarrelled with Rome, and Henry VIII's row with the Pope over his divorce from Katherine of Aragon, and even his despoiling of the monasteries, would not necessarily have led to the establishment of a National Church in a different age. The idea of the Church of England really got under way in the reigns of his children. Under his son Edward VI, there emerged two Prayer Books – vernacular liturgies: the first, of 1549, closely based on the old Roman Mass, and the second, of 1552, much more Protestant. Under Edward VI's sister Queen Elizabeth, the Settlement of the Church of England became more fixed, a liturgy closely based on that of 1552 was established as the Common Prayer of the Realm, and the Church was increasingly seen as an essential part of the self-confident independent nation-state which England had become. Crown and Church were inextricably linked. Not merely did the Queen appoint the bishops, but Queen and bishops between them shared a view of what the Church was, and what its place was in the life of the nation.

Those Christians who dread Erastianism would have a particular horror of the Elizabethan Settlement and the subsequent development of the Church of England. Viewed from another perspective, however, the Church of England could be seen as a sanctifying thread, woven through the entire texture of national life. The whole of England was divided into parishes. Every soul in that parish was the responsibility of the parish priest – even if as individuals they expressed beliefs which were quite different from those of the established faith. Morning and evening, the parson would ring the bell to read Morning and Evening Prayer, with, or on behalf of, his people. The Church of England ideal was an inclusive, not an exclusive, ideal. The doctrinally scrupulous attacked it, Calvinists because it retained too much of the old Catholic structures – for example, the threefold ministry of bishop, priest and deacon; Roman Catholics likewise attacked it for its doctrinal vagueness, its lack of apparently Catholic intention in its ordinal, its apparent lack of Eucharistic theology in the Thirty-Nine Articles.

Yet the Church of England took root and, though perhaps it never was quite what its early defenders, such as Richard Hooker, desired, it did remain deep into the nineteenth century a unique part of national life. Enthusiasts for it, such as Gladstone, seem like bigots to us today, with their unwillingness to grant emancipation – the franchise, a career at the Bar, or a University degree – to Nonconformists and Roman Catholics and Jews. Their ideal was in one sense intensely narrow-minded and in another extraordinarily wide: they believed that to be English, and to believe in God, naturally qualified you for membership of the national Church. Why go elsewhere, when you were already, under God, a member of this 'blessed company'; when you already, whether or not you recognised it as a fact, belonged to a parish; there was already a font to baptise your children, a register in which your marriage and death would be recorded, an altar from which you could be sacramentally fed, and a churchyard in which you could be buried? This ideal, in a way which was not logical but empirical and factual, had little by little been bound tightly to the concept of Monarchy.

When James VI of Scotland became James I of England in 1603, and summoned the Hampton Court Conference to debate the future of the national Church, it was put to him by a Protestant representative that they should abolish the episcopate. He made his famous exclamation: 'Thus, I take it – no bishop, no king!' The phrase was much on everyone's lips a generation later, when the extreme Protestants of the victorious Parliamentary side, led by Oliver Cromwell, insisted upon the execution of Charles I. Whatever his faults as a King and as a war leader, there can be no doubt of Charles's piety. He was the first English Monarch to be brought up from the cradle as a member of the Church of England, and he certainly saw his own death as a form of martyrdom. Among other things, he died for the Book of Common Prayer and for the bishops. When, after eleven years of republicanism, the English restored the Monarchy, it was automatically, and correctly, assumed that the Church of England would be also restored, together with its bishops, priests and deacons. Thereafter, the Monarchy and the Church were inextricably linked, and it has been a curious fact that on the two occasions since, when it was found necessary to get rid of the Sovereign, the instrument for doing so was religious: both James II and Edward VIII had to go because of their unwillingness to conform to the Church of England.

Many of those who watched the Queen's Coronation on television in 1953 would have been struck by the intensely religious nature of the occasion. After the great officers of State – the Archbishop of Canterbury, Garter King of Arms, the Lord Chancellor, the Lord Chamberlain and the Earl Marshal – had presented the Queen to her people, and the fanfare of trumpets had blasted out, the Queen took her Coronation Oath. She promised in that oath to govern her peoples in all their lands according to their respective laws and customs; to cause law and justice in mercy to be executed in all her judgements; and then, more controversially, she promised to 'maintain the laws of God and the true profession of the Gospel, to maintain in the United Kingdom the Protestant Reformed Religion established by law, to maintain and preserve inviolably the settlement of the Church of England and the doctrine, worship, discipline and government thereof'.

There then followed the Communion service, and what – to some eyes – must have seemed the highly un-Protestant ceremony of anointing, in which the Queen was consecrated wearing sacred vestments – the *colobium sindonis* (a white, sleeveless surplice), the *supertunica*, a close-fitting surcoat almost indistinguishable from a deacon's dalmatic. When she had been thus arrayed, the Queen had a sword placed in her right hand by the Archbishop and he spoke to her these words: 'With this sword do justice, stop the growth of iniquity, protect the holy Church of God, help and defend widows and orphans, restore the things that are gone to decay, maintain the things that are restored . . .'

It is a beguilingly conservative picture of the Monarch's religious and civil functions. It is a little more difficult, looking at Great Britain forty years after the Coronation, to see the reality to which these symbolic gestures were supposed to correspond. There are more practising Moslems in Great Britain than there are Methodists. Among the Christian denominations, by far the most flourishing is the Roman Catholic Church, which accounts for about half the church-going population of the country.

Among Anglicans (as members of the Church of England almost always seem to call themselves nowadays, as though they were merely, like other English Christians, members of a 'denomination') there are many who question the value or morality of Establishment. Since 1970 the Church of England has had its own Parliament, known as the General Synod. With this Parliament they have thrown out the Prayer Book which was the sign and focus of unity in the national Church. They replaced it with a new 'Alternative Service Book' (1980) but, in reality, there is no more 'Common Prayer' in the English Church. Some follow the Alternative Book; many make up their own rites or follow the missals of Rome. The Church of England is in a state of liturgical anarchy since it chose to manage its own affairs, and since its decision to ordain women to the priesthood (1992) it would appear to have lost its semblance of unity. Both the Archbishops of Canterbury and York have said that the Coronation Oath must be changed, and they have hinted that they are not really happy that the Church of England (if it may still be said to exist) should be the Established Religion. Princess Margaret and a few of her friends might choose to believe that the Queen derives her authority from God, and that the Church of England derives its deserved supremacy over all other religions directly from the Queen. But in reality it is hard to see how the Established Religion can retain any sort of plausibility when fewer than five per cent of the population claim to adhere to it.

When the Prime Minister rose to tell the House of Commons on December 9, 1992, that the Prince of Wales was to separate from his wife, he caused considerable astonishment by stating that this would not stop the Princess being crowned Queen at some future date. Gasps were heard in the Chamber. The astonishment was partly caused by the sheer unlikeliness of such a ceremony ever taking place – the new King arriving at the Abbey in one carriage, the new Queen in another, before departing, presumably, to their separate palaces to receive the adulation of separate crowds. But the idea of the Prince of Wales and his wife ascending the throne awakened memories of Edward VIII who, because of his honest desire to marry the woman he loved, a woman who had been married before, was prepared to abandon the throne. Of course, Mr Major had not said that if the Prince divorced his wife she could still be the Queen; but the idea of a 'legally separated' King and Queen came close to this unthinkable ideal.

Surely the marital status of the new King or Queen – whoever they turn out to be – is only a small part of what makes us gasp if we actually contemplate any future Coronation ceremony. Can the Head of State of a country which is eighty per cent irreligious, five per cent non-Christian religions and five per cent Roman Catholic persist in holding a sword in his or her hand and promising to maintain the 'Protestant Reformed Religion established by law'? In all probability, by the time of the next Coronation it will not be established by law. Quite possibly a large section of those who dislike the ordination of women to the priesthood will, on this ground alone, have separated themselves from the Established Church and either joined the Roman Church or formed a new sect of their own. In these circumstances in which 'things fall apart', it is hard to see how the monarchical 'centre' can hold.

Or is this another case, like the political sphere, where the Monarchy can survive without any function or status whatsoever? It is actually quite hard to see how this could be. Even if they are meaningless to the majority of those who hear them, the words of the Coronation Oath still have to be spoken, and in the multi-cultural, multi-ethnic, multi-denominational Britain in which the Sovereign now finds herself it is hard to see how they could be spoken, for the more sincerely they were spoken, the more offensive they would seem.

There is of course no need to have Coronation Services at all. The Queen became the Queen automatically on the death of her father, and when the appropriate proclamations and oaths had been made that day, on her return to London from Kenya, she did not have to wait fifteen months – from February 1952 when the King died, to June 1953 when she was crowned – to call herself Queen. Her ancestor William IV wanted to forgo a Coronation Service altogether; this was because he believed the ostentation of his brother's Coronation only ten years before had been shocking. In spite of his irregular habits, William IV was a devout man who died with the mysterious words 'The Church! The Church!' on his lips. One can have Kings without Coronations, and one can have Anglican Churches without the Establishment, as the Anglican Churches all over the world – in Wales, Ireland, the United States, Australia and Africa – have shown.

Nevertheless, when these facts come to be recognised on the Statute Book and the appropriate changes are made by the Westminster Parliament, there is no doubt that they will be seen as a further weakening of the House of Windsor. Bagehot believed that Queen Victoria exercised a religious role in society, and in her strange way she probably did. (Not that she was a very keen Anglican;

when Archbishop Benson told her that he did not like her receiving the Sacrament in the Scottish Church while she was north of the border in Balmoral, she reminded him that, while the Church of England was the Established Church in England, the Church of Scotland (Presbyterian) was the established Church there. The Archbishop had no authority in Scotland, and the Queen had. Henceforth she excommunicated herself from the Church of England and, though she continued to be its supreme Governor, she did not receive its sacraments.

Probably, Queen Elizabeth II, with her taste for unfussy ceremonial and her simple, Bible-based Christianity, is happier to worship at Crathie parish church, near Balmoral, than she would be in some of the more exalted Anglo-Catholic fanes in London, such as Holy Trinity, Sloane Street, favoured by her racier sister. If the Queen visited the Shrine of Our Lady of Walsingham, much favoured by the Duchess of Kent, she might respond as her grandfather George V did when he saw it – 'Is this *my* church?' Prince Philip, who has done his best to be a loyal Anglican since his marriage, and has befriended such figures as the Dean of Windsor, the Very Reverend Michael Mann, has now reverted to the Greek Orthodoxy which was his parents' religion.

It looks increasingly unrealistic to insist that the Royal Family should be the upholders of the Church of England. But it leaves them with a problem. For if they are not, as George V and George VI would have maintained, the firm upholders of monogamous, Church of England faith and life, what is their function? If the Monarch's connection with the Church does not matter, and if the Establishment of the Church can be discarded without shaking the fabric of things, why was it necessary to send Edward VIII into exile? The Queen Mother might have an answer to this, but few others would. If the Windsors are no longer fit to be icons of happily married life – because of their unhappy marital history – and if their religious beliefs are not even upheld within their own household – let alone shared by more than five per cent of the population of Great Britain – does it not follow that their function, if they have one at all, is diminished? No longer Defenders of the Faith, and no longer Ideals of Family Virtue, the Monarchs of the future – if such there be – will exercise a purely constitutional role.

NINE

Constitutional Monarchy

'What must the king do now? Must he submit?'
Shakespeare, *Richard II*

In his recent book on the Constitution, Ferdinand Mount*
noted a perceptible change in the way that the Royal Family
appeared to regard their public role. They have begun to
speak out about issues of the day in a way which would have
been regarded as 'undue' interference in the days, let us say,
when Edward VIII said that 'something must be done' about
the plight of the unemployed in South Wales in 1936. Mr
Mount lists the Princess Royal lamenting the shortage of
services for the under-fives and urging the Government
to match the level of facilities available on the Continent,
and Prince Philip deriding the environmental ignorance
of 'the cloistered precincts of the schools of monetary
economists'. And there has been a whole series of comments on public matters by the Prince of Wales: his protest
against inadequate Government spending on the care of the

The British Constitution Now (1992).

154

elderly, and his attacks on modern architects. Mount says, 'The really remarkable thing is that nobody – nobody at all, whether on the constitutionalist right or the socialist left – seems to have felt like uttering a peep of protest. The sort of royal opinion which only ten or twenty years ago would have had the media clucking about a constitutional crisis is now taken for granted as a natural element in public debate.'

Those words appeared in 1992, and they already seem very slightly out of date. Since Mr Mount's book was published, there has been the crisis of the GATT talks, in which the quarrel between the United States and the French farmers over the subject of rape-seed oil threatened the future economic stability of the world. As was explained in Chapter Three, at the most delicate moment of the negotiations the Prince of Wales, on a visit to France, declared himself wholeheartedly on the side of the French farmers.

Mr Mount offers two justifications for Royals speaking out on public matters, or at least an explanation for why the public might tolerate such outbursts. In the first place, he says, 'self-expression has become an article of faith. Virtually everyone now seems to be in a position to answer back.' In the second place, Royal persons are merely exercising in public the right they used to exercise in private, 'to be consulted, to encourage, to warn' – the old 'rights' attributed to Queen Victoria by Bagehot.

While this might conceivably apply to the Princess Royal wishing that there were better nursery facilities in English towns, it all begins to look rather different in a case such as the Prince of Wales's intervention in the GATT dispute. Here we have a case of the British Government, its Foreign Office and its Treasury, taking one view, and the Prince of Wales (son of the Head of State, and potential Head of State) taking another. Supposing he had made his intervention when he was actually King, which would have constituted the view of His Majesty's Government? Is this the taste of things to come – a Monarch who will not be content to be consulted, to encourage and to warn? Are we entering another phase of British history when, to use Bagehot's memorable phrase to describe George III, 'we have the case of a meddling maniac'? In constitutional terms, all this matters much more than whether the Prince of Wales has 'talked dirty' on the telephone with the wife of a brother officer. 'George III interfered unceasingly, but he did harm unceasingly' – Bagehot again.

No one questions that the Prince of Wales is perfectly within his rights to make comments about any matter which he chooses. Not only is he a free individual, but, as Duke of Cornwall, he is a member of the House of Lords, and he is every bit as entitled as any other peer of the realm to make pronouncements about the important issues of the day. Moreover, this is an area where, surprisingly enough, the Royal Family have neither declined nor fallen in public esteem.

British politicians are held by the public at large in a derision and contempt which it would be impossible to overestimate and difficult for a foreigner to comprehend. Bagehot wrote at a time when politicians enjoyed a measure of public esteem, and when some of them, such as Gladstone and Disraeli, were extremely popular. Parliament was vigorous, and franchise was still a recent privilege for the majority of the British male population; for the female population it was still an unrealised dream. It was small wonder, then, that he should have supposed that the glory of England was its Parliament and that 'when we look at history, we shall find that it is only during the period of the present reign that in England the duties of the constitutional sovereign have ever been well performed'. What he meant by this was that the politicians of the high Victorian era were giants who entirely overshadowed their Monarch; and that though Queen Victoria did make periodic attempts to interfere in political life, especially in the area of foreign affairs, she was generally much too lazy to follow in the footsteps of her grandfather, the 'meddling maniac'.

After more than a decade with a Prime Minister who belonged very decidedly to the Meddling Maniac school, the British people have had a surfeit of politicians. The present Prime Minister, Mr Major, is said by the opinion polls to be the least popular since such information was first collected, and the same would undoubtedly be true whoever occupied this office and whichever party were in power. In such a circumstance there is undoubtedly a vacuum in British political life, and in different circumstances this vacuum could obviously be filled by some members of the Royal Family.

This is not to indulge in royalist fantasy. Few would wish for an absolutist Monarchy in Britain. But there is a basis of ill will (against politicians) in Britain upon which the Royal Family could certainly have capitalised. At the beginning of this book it was suggested that the overwhelming presidential style of Margaret Thatcher left the British public winded, and the Monarchy somewhat overshadowed. But in the right climate this would have counted, eventually, to the benefit of the Royal Family. It may do so yet. But the *annus horribilis* was the one year in the family's history when they could have done without any breath of scandal.

This was a year in which scandals of one sort or another clung to the Government. Cabinet Ministers were exposed in the Press for the seedy lot they are: one of them inadvertently rented his basement to a prostitute, and no one except himself could see why it had been necessary for him to borrow over £20,000 from public funds for having her evicted. Another Minister of the Crown confessed to having a steamy affair with an actress on a mattress in Earls Court. The newspapers made much of the fact that toe-sucking had formed part of this strange liaison. If ever there were a year in which the Royal Family could have been well advised not to indulge in toe-sucking, it was this one. Unfortunately, the Duchess of York could not resist allowing her feet to be kissed by her financial adviser, thereby giving the tabloid Press the chance to make all these public figures – royalties and politicians – equally clownish, equally base in the eyes of the public. But when the toe-sucking has stopped or been forgotten, when Prince Charles's extremely embarrassing telephone calls to the wife of Silver Stick in Waiting have been consigned to oblivion, are the British still capable of taking the Monarchy seriously? Does the idea of a constitutional Monarchy still have a place in modern Britain – multi-cultural, multi-ethnic Britain, Britain the somewhat grudging member of the EC, Britain the not-so-popular satellite of the United States? What does the Queen do? Why do the English in particular, and the British in general, retain a monarchical system of government? How much is the Queen still a serious part of the political scene, and how far is she merely a decorative figure?

There are no easy answers to these questions. How you answer them depends on the angle from which you are looking. Rather than attempt a definition, it would probably be better to look at the Monarchy from several angles, just as one might study different elevations of a single building. One way of exploring the constitutional position of the British Monarchy is to answer the question: how might it be abolished? Not 'How could you get rid of one Monarch and replace them with another?', but 'How could you get rid of the Monarchy?' I do not posit this question in an emotive manner, and I do not suggest that it *should* be abolished. I am asking the question as a way of discovering what part is still played by the Crown in British national life. It will be found when one asks this question that Monarchy, and the concept of Monarchy, is interwoven with the fabric of British life at many levels, and one could not merely get rid of the Monarchy without changing many other things as well. The Monarchy is not just a golden bauble on the top of a stone pyramid; it is more like the golden thread running through an entire tapestry. Unpick it, and much more than the thread itself would be lost.

Or such would have been the case until fifty years ago. Another way of viewing the whole matter would be to suggest that Monarchy was an inherent and inextricable part of a structure of society and a *realpolitik* which has already changed; that as the British wrestle with, or discard, the old class structures of society and the parliamentary tradition of government, it is inevitable that the Monarchy itself will be threatened. Whichever way you regard it, the Crown is very much more than simply the person who happens to be wearing it, and its significance transcends the personalities of the Royal Family.

Viewed from the most extreme monarchist position, the idea of abolishing Monarchies is self-contradictory. No one possesses such authority, since the power of Kings comes from God. When Charles I was put on trial in Westminster Hall in January 1649, he protested against the very legality of the proceedings with the words, 'If it were my own particular case, I would have satisfied myself with the protestation I made the last time I was here against the legality of the Court, and that a King cannot be tried by any superior jurisdiction on earth. But it is not in my case alone, it is the freedom and the liberty of the people of England; and do you pretend what you will, I stand for their liberties. For if power without law may make laws, may alter the fundamental laws of the kingdom, I do not know what subject he is in England, that can be sure of his life or anything that he calls his own.' In the course of the trial, Bradshaw, the President of the Court, asserted that 'the King is but an officer in trust, and he ought to discharge that trust'. It was Charles's failure to discharge that trust to the Court's satisfaction which led to the King's condemnation and beheading.

The debate about the function of the Monarchy was to continue during the next thirty years until the Revolution of 1688–9 which sent Charles I's son James into exile. Cromwell in the Protectorate had never sufficiently answered the King's fundamental question – how is it possible outside a Monarchy to maintain an independent judiciary and legislative system and to protect individual citizens, by means of the law, against the encroachments of power? Charles maintained that the Crown and the judiciary between them were a safeguard, which a Republican government could never be. Cromwell might have seen himself as King in all but name, as 'an officer in trust', to use Bradshaw's definition of kingship. But the eleven-year Republican experiment in England from 1649 to 1660 was an illustration of how true Charles I's words had been at his trial. Ruling sometimes by overt military means – as during the spell of government by the Major-Generals – and sometimes by covert military power, Cromwell replaced monarchy with dictatorship. After the Restoration of Charles II in 1660, there were tensions between a monarchist perception of the Divine Right and a Parliamentary stressing of the civic duty of Kings. The Revolutionary settlement of 1689 was very largely a compromise between these two positions. It would seem illogical, but it has gradually evolved into a workable system. Those who look askance at the inequalities which are an essential part of any monarchical system must face the conundrum contained in Charles I's protest to his prosecutors. Power in the political sphere, like energy in the physical sphere, is not something which will vanish. If it is not harnessed in one way, it will be harnessed in another.

Monarchy is one such check on the unlimited power of Parliaments or of Cabinets, or of juntas or of autocrats. Since this check has been an inbuilt part of the system in Britain since 1689, there are only two ways in which the Monarchy could be abolished. The first – more or less unthinkable in the present political climate – is a revolution or *coup d'état* such as deposed Charles I in 1649 or Louis XVI in 1789. The only other way in which the British Monarchy could be abolished would be if it were to abolish itself, by ratifying a Parliamentary Bill which brought the Monarchy to an end. This would involve the Prime Minister coming to the dispatch box of the House of Commons and proposing the motion that Great Britain should be a republic. In the present climate, this would be so profoundly unpopular, both in the House and in the country at large, that it would be very unlikely to happen; but if such a proposal were to be passed through the House of Commons and be drafted as a Bill, it would then have to be sent to the Upper House for approval. In the very unlikely event of such a Bill being approved in the House of Lords and passing all the various Committee Stages in both Houses, it would then be sent to the Sovereign to be ratified. He or she would then discharge his or her last office of State by abolishing the Crown. Such an Alice-in-Wonderland fantasy would be extremely unlikely to come to pass in any foreseeable British Parliament.

But let us imagine that the Republic were established. By so doing, Parliament would also abolish the system of patronage, it would abolish the system of Royal preroga-tive whereby the Queen can exercise power outright, and it would abolish the Monarch's ability to ratify Bills. It would be unrealistic to suppose, merely because the Crown had been removed from Elizabeth Windsor's head, that the network which thrives upon and feeds the system of patronage would disappear overnight. We are not here talking just about who gets particular awards in the Birth-day Honours list. Patronage as an idea runs through the whole of British public life, which is why thoroughgoing democrats and republicans like Mr Tony Benn wish to abolish it. Administrative tribunals, advisory bodies, the Civil Service, the judiciary, justices of the peace, the major ecclesiastical appointments, some of the more prestigious academic appointments, are all tied up with the system of patronage, and they all depend, at least notionally, upon the Crown. Such a system cannot be abolished overnight; it can merely be handled more or less corruptly.

Idealists would like to believe that, once the Crown and the class system and the 'old-boy network' were done away with, the system would become freer, more honest, more accountable. Such an optimistic view would not seem to be justified by a study either of human nature or of the systems of government which obtain throughout the world. The laborious manner in which new administrations come and go (not always without corruption) in the United States would have to provide the British with a role model. It is hard to see why they would be tempted to substitute their creakingly archaic, but workable, system for one which, however it were devised, would not necessarily be any more efficient or more just.

The existence of a Royal Prerogative dismays some demo-crats. For example, while Members of Parliament were debating the Maastricht Treaty, it was pointed out to them that it did not require the yea or nay of Parliament to ratify a treaty. It was only a courtesy that they were being consulted at all. Treaties with other nations are ratified not by Parliament, but by the Sovereign. There was an outcry at this, but there should not have been. It was a reminder of how responsibly and sensibly the Royal Prerogative has been exercised over the last fifty years, and what a useful check it has placed on potential power-maniacs in No. 10 Downing Street. When the Prerogative is in the hands of an hereditary Monarch, there can exist the principle that Parliament must be consulted on matters of national importance. This is partly a democratic principle, partly a looser thing, based on that notion of 'consensus' which has been at the basis of the Windsors' political education. Imagine what use Margaret Thatcher would have made of Presidential Prerogative had she been the head of a British Republic in the days of her fullest power and vigour!

Such a comparison might make us suppose that the Queen has no power. But the Sovereign is devoid of power only in the sense that the Queen herself is not a dictator. She is not devoid of power if you imagine this power being transferred from her hands to those of anyone else. Constitutional Monarchy provides, as the Spanish have found, an extremely effective non-democratic means of controlling the power of the State. It is as different as possible from dictatorship, since its power is used to check and to control rather than to tyrannise.

The Constitutional Sovereign occupies a position as Head of State which is comparable to that of a leaseholder of real estate. The leaseholder purchases the right to occupy a particular property for a fixed period but, when the lease is finished, the ownership of the property reverts to the freeholder. This analogy does not fit the case in every particular, but it is truer, as a picture of things, than to suppose that the British Sovereign exercises a purely independent authority. Had they been absolute Monarchs (as perhaps they would have liked to be), James II would not have been dispatched from his realm in 1688, and Edward VIII would not have been sent to France in 1936.

The principles of 1689, when William of Orange and his wife Mary (sister of James II) were offered the Crown by the Lords and Commons of England, held strong for 250 years. There was no need for a written 'lease' agreement between Sovereign and people, because everyone knew the rules. Britain was governed by an oligarchy, and this ruling class remained dominant from 1689 until the outbreak of the Second World War. This is not to say that during the nineteenth century there had not been a gradual extension of franchise. But, when you look at the composition of successive British Governments during this period, no one can be in any doubt where the real power in Great Britain actually resided. It resided with the oligarchy – or the upper class. The great landed and monied families ensured that the Establishment ran the country – beneath the aristocracy, the Civil Service and the professional classes, most of whom were educated at private schools, who spoke and dressed in a manner which differentiated them from the rest of the people. Into this scheme of things, the Constitutional Monarchy fitted very well, and it was when the Constitutional Monarchy came under threat that two other views of Monarchy resurrected themselves: the spirit of 1649 and the spirit of 1715.

In 1649, Charles I, having lost the Civil War against the Parliamentarians, walked to his death on a scaffold which had been set up outside the Banqueting Hall in Whitehall. For the next eleven years England was a Republic, for most of this period under the Protectorate of Oliver Cromwell. Republicanism of this out-and-out character –

known to its adherents as the Good Old Cause – knew some fine defenders: the poet John Milton was perhaps its most eloquent spokesman in the seventeenth century; Tom Paine in the eighteenth century. After the aristocratic *coup* of 1689, however, which neutered both the power of the people and the power of the Monarch, and kept power firmly in the hands of the oligarchy, there was little hope that republicanism would take root in England.

The case altered in the twentieth century with the arrival of universal suffrage, but strangely enough the British Labour movement, though it has always carried republicans in its midst, was never strongly republican in flavour in its purer socialist days. The former railwayman J. H. Thomas, the first Labour Colonial Secretary, became one of King George V's best friends. When one reads accounts of Ramsay Macdonald, it is striking how afraid the first Socialist Cabinet were of the corruption of snobbery; rightly, as it turned out. A Labour 'incorruptible' asked the Prime Minister why he could not go to Buckingham Palace, and Macdonald replied, 'Because its allurements are so great that I cannot trust you to go.'* He meant it. No doubt snobbery, which is no less prevalent on the left wing of the political spectrum than on the right, has saved the British people from more sinister alliances between the Sovereign and forces of the extremes. For snobbery is one of the small things in life which inspires even political ideologues to want the system to continue much as it is; and this desire has always been strong, even in the parties of reform – whether Whig, Liberal, or Labour.

The opposite of Constitutional Monarchy would be the extreme right-wing wish that British Monarchs should be absolute rulers in the Bourbon mould. '*L'état, c'est moi.*' The

*Kenneth Rose, *George V* (1983) p.331.

two major attempts in the eighteenth century to restore the Stuart dynasty – the rebellions of 1715 and 1745 – were the most romantic expressions of this view. In the first three decades of the twentieth century, those on the extreme right came to believe that an Absolute Monarchy was the only system of government which protected the people from the ravages of the Money Power (a euphemism in most such writings for the Jews). The most eloquent English (or half-English) exponent of such an opinion in the 1930s was perhaps Hilaire Belloc; Maurras in France took a comparable view. They saw the new dictators, such as Dr Salazar, General Franco and Signor Mussolini, as absolute monarchs come again to wrest power from the plutocrats and hold it, in sacred trust from on high, on behalf of their people. It was perhaps harder to take quite such a neo-mediaeval view of Herr Hitler, though there were those, such as G. K. Chesterton's cousin, A. K. Chesterton, who tried. There would seem to be some evidence, in spite of his protestations of belief in the constitutional principles of George V, that Edward VIII inclined to this view of the Monarch's rule. Certainly Hitler and his immediate associates were given to understand by von Ribbentrop that, in the event of a German victory in 1940, Edward VIII and his Duchess would be installed as the Nazi puppet King and Queen; we do not know whether they would have accepted such a role had it been offered to them. No doubt the Fascist sympathies of the King and his friends – such as the Metcalfes, the Mosleys et al. – helped to alarm the Establishment, and it was convenient when he fell in love with a divorced woman for them to get rid of him on non-political grounds. But the Jacobite or Absolutist idea of Monarchy has never had many adherents in England since 1649, and probably not in Scotland since the Battle of Flodden in 1513. Like the Good Old Cause, the devotion to the King Over The Water has been the luxury of a few eccentrics.

The principle of 1689 was what kept the Monarchy alive and made it plausible. Those who still believe in the Good Old Cause and wish to get rid of the Monarchy's power would point to the fact that the British Sovereign exercises more than a purely symbolic function. As we have seen, every Member of Parliament, every civil servant, every bishop, must make an oath of obedience to the Sovereign.

It is true that all legislation passed through the Houses of Parliament has to be signed and ratified by the Royal Assent. And the Monarch spends much of her time with 'boxes', signing documents. But (and this is the fact to which Mr Benn and the Good Old Causers perhaps give insufficient attention) she would be gravely mistaken if she thought that her 'assent' could be withheld from any item of legislation without a major rumpus, and she would almost certainly find if she chose to oppose some law or act that the Houses of Parliament made her think again. A deliberately orchestrated clash between the Crown and the Commons over a serious matter of public policy is now, in the reign of Elizabeth II, so unthinkable that it would never actually happen. To that extent she is a rubber stamp, just as the Queen's Speech is a semi-farcical ritual in which she announces from the throne a set of policies which have been written down by whichever politicians have just won the General Election.

The system, however, began to break down long ago with the dissolution of the old governing class, and it was really a series of accidents which disguised from the British people – and, one suspects, from the Sovereign herself – the fact that she is a leaseholder whose landlord no longer exists. The symbiosis of monarchy and aristocracy which insured that the system worked properly has now gone.

This has had the effect of neutering the Monarchy. It also means that since there is no one truly empowered to sack the Monarch, so there is no one usefully empowered to advise or counsel or support the Sovereign. One very obvious fact about the present Royal Family, when you compare them with, let us say, the children of George III, is how few people they really know. This was made worse by Prince Philip's desire to educate his sons at an eccentric German school in Scotland rather than sending them – if they were sent to school at all – to Eton. True, they have met people since, in the Navy and in hunting parties. But had Prince Charles been at Eton, he would have known half London. Eton would have provided him with ready-made links, just like the old aristocratic houses in London in which George III's sons, the wastrel Royal Dukes, 'knew' people. To this extent it has been of more importance, politically, for the Prince of Wales to make friends than for the Queen. It is to be hoped that more care is taken over his sons' education than was taken over his own. It is simply essential that they be sent to Eton, for it is only by 'knowing people' on a wide scale that the Sovereign's power can be exercised usefully in the future.

There are those who would say that the Maastricht Treaty represents a neutering of the power and function of the Crown. For example, it would be by no means clear, were anyone to attempt to put this treaty into effect, whether the Sovereign was still head of the Armed Forces or whether she retained the power to make or unmake laws. Such powers as these would seem to have been deferred to Brussels Eurocrats or passed to the European Parliaments. How much this would matter in practice will remain to be seen. There are so many other imponderables about Maastricht that this might be thought to be the least of the difficulties of those attempting to put it all into effect. Taking the Foreign Office line, the Queen went to the European Parliament and said that she was wholeheartedly in favour of the Maastricht Treaty. The frivolous reason for this might be supposed that she was bored by having to sign all those State papers, and was perfectly happy to pass the chore to a Eurocrat. The emotional reasons are probably much deeper and stronger. No British family has so many continental (and particularly so many German) connections, and she might well feel that this is a matter close to her personally. It is very much the sort of thing Prince Albert and Edward VII would have approved.

If Sovereignty itself technically passed to Europe, and the religious significance of Monarchy was changed or eradicated – what would be the function of the Crown in British life? By curtailing the Sovereign's power yet further by Maastricht, it is harder than ever to be a Jacobite. The men of 1649 (many of them opposed to Maastricht for different reasons) would nonetheless say that this is the moment for Britain to become a republic. If politics were ever decided according to logical principles, this would quite possibly take place. But there is of course nothing logical about these matters, and the Sovereign might well survive without having a reason to survive.

The new development has been the call from serious Westminster Parliamentarians for a reform of the Monarchy. Hitherto, as we have seen, republicans or radicals who dared to criticise the Royal Family were always relegated to the status of clowns by the Parliamentary Labour Party because it was known that to allow the party as a whole to be tarred with the republican brush would be electorally disastrous. In the recent Parliament, however, even though the Leader of the Labour Party has tried to restrain them there have been a considerable number of

Labour MPs supporting the calls by such as Mo Mowlem and Roy Hattersley (no Marxists they) for a 'reformed Monarchy'. These views have also been echoed in some of the more killjoy areas of the Liberal benches.

Perhaps the most senior politician to support the call for reform is Mr Hattersley, the former deputy leader of the Labour Party. In a long article in the *Observer*,* he opined that 'it is preposterous that, in the last decade of the twentieth century, Parliament should be regaled with assurances about the rights of succession'. It is hard to see why the late twentieth century should be a better or worse time than any other to discuss the rights of succession to the British Crown. But, according to Hattersley, 'the whole idea of inherited authority is innately unreasonable'. It is based on what Bagehot called 'mystic reverence' and 'religious allegiance'. Needless to say, Hattersley feels the need to repeat that 'neither of these emotions is appropriate to the last decades of the twentieth century'. His article concludes that, however much 'reform' the Queen introduces, 'a republic is one day inevitable'. The paradox is, of course, that even after its most disastrous year since the Abdication, the British Monarchy is infinitely more popular than the Labour Party. Given the democratic choice, whether to choose a President like Mr Hattersley or to continue with the present system, the British would vote in droves for the Queen. It is for this reason – the rather self-contradictory fact that the British Monarchy is democratically popular – that it remains politically important. Because most British people wish it to continue, it is essential that it continues to adapt itself to the political, social and religious realities of the day. If it needs to change and adapt, and to be quarrelled about and debated, that is precisely because it is alive, not because,

*December 13, 1992.

as Hattersley implies, it is moribund. Meanwhile, of course, Hattersley and his like will bring before Parliament all kinds of plans to 'streamline' or 'modernise' the Monarchy, and, since they are politicians, the subject uppermost in their minds will be money.

TEN

Royal Money

'What does she do with it?'
Graffito seen by Gladstone

When Norman Hartnell, the Queen's dressmaker, died, there was a flurry among all the grand couturiers in London. Was this, I asked one of them, because they were all so anxious to make dresses for the Queen Mother and the Queen? Not at all. They all dreaded the commission. When I asked why, I was told that the Queen Mother had seldom been known to pay a bill in her life. 'The Queen, of course,' said my informant, 'pays on the nail. But we have not had the heart to tell her that prices have risen somewhat since 1947.'

If the House of Windsor has aroused envy and rancour in the populace at large, one has to concede that it is partly because of their greed and their meanness. Any formal public analysis of the riches of the Queen or her family fails to take account of what they claim by way of expenses. In this regard, they could give a lesson to the most cynical of journalists or lawyers. Every time the

Queen or her husband travels abroad, a bill for travelling expenses is sent to the British Embassy of the country which she or he happens to be visiting. This bill will include the price of Prince Philip's suits and ties and shirts, the Queen's outfits and the clothes worn by all their equerries and ladies-in-waiting. No ambassador ever questions the bills, which are often enormous. They are sent back to the Foreign Office in London, and paid by the taxpayer. Since the Queen and the Duke of Edinburgh spend a substantial part of each year travelling, they could be said to live on 'expenses'. These vast sums never appear in any account of what the Royal Family costs the British taxpayer.

At a time when many British people have been feeling poor, the Royal Family has not hesitated to flaunt its great personal wealth. The most glaring, and ugly, example of this is the ranch-style dwelling, built for a sum in excess of £5 million on the edge of Windsor Great Park, for Prince Andrew to live in with his unfaithful wife. Since that marriage lasted less than five years, this hideous dwelling may be said to have cost the Queen a million pounds a year.

One could write a lengthy and tedious catalogue of the greed of the Windsors. The Queen Mother's gambling addictions, and the high sums she has wasted on injudicious wagers, would alone fill a book. The question remains, however, whether a discussion of Royal money should hinge upon the Windsors' moral failings or whether it should try to ask the more delicate question of what, and whose, the Royal money is. What principles, if any, govern the thinking of politicians and journalists about this matter? Is it simply envy of the Windsors' wealth and distaste for the way they spend it? If so – bring on the tumbrils! Or is it a confused sense of contract? A muddle about what Royal ownership – let us say of a palace or a castle – means?

Nearly all the quarrels which the English people have had with their Kings and Queens have been to do with money. In the past, a Monarch's revenue was raised through taxation. Charles I, for example, did not, like a modern rich man, have an 'investment portfolio' to help him indulge his taste for fine paintings. He bought all those Rubenses and Van Dycks and Titians out of taxpayers' money – because this, apart from rents on Royal lands, was the chief source of his income. The modern distinction between 'private wealth' and 'State wealth', between the personal property of Charles Stuart and the property of 'the Crown', would have been meaningless to the Royal Martyr. Parliament wished to keep to itself the right to grant the King money through tax revenue – one of the great causes of dispute between them when the King exercised his ancient privilege of raising Ship Money without reference to Parliament. In the days when English Kings aspired to absolute power, they were dependent on their people to supply that power to give them the money to raise armies and to build their palaces. Paradoxically, it is in the twentieth century, when the Royal House is almost devoid of political power, that the Kings and Queens have enjoyed enormous independent wealth. If the Queen's Civil List payment were stopped tomorrow, she could survive on a personal basis – but of course it would remain open to question whether the Monarchy could survive.

Many seemingly wise words are written nowadays about the Queen and her money. Lawyers and tax experts and politicians pontificate wisely about property which belongs to 'the State' and property which belongs to Her Majesty in a private capacity, but their words do not make much sense. The great difference between the House of Windsor and the House of Stuart is that the Windsors are indeed extremely rich in a private capacity. This notion of the 'private capacity' was developed during the reign of Queen Victoria, who managed to cream off a tidy fortune from her income from the Civil List and the Privy Purse. She learnt this trick from her Uncle Leopold, later King of the Belgians: he was briefly husband of Princess Charlotte, 'Prince Consort', a role for which the British Parliament voted him £1 million annually for life, and which he continued to draw long after the demise of his beloved Princess. Balmoral was built with what Victoria and Prince Albert regarded as 'our own money'. And, from the same source, Sandringham House in Norfolk, with a fine estate, became the personal property of her son, the Prince of Wales.

Nineteenth-century newspapers habitually carped at the money which the Royal Family spent on their houses. The extravagance of George IV is something for which posterity is grateful – since it gave us, among other glories, Brighton Pavilion, the remodelled Windsor Castle and the renovated Buckingham Palace. At the time, the Press and Parliament only minded about the money – £1 million spent on the refurbishment of Buckingham Palace alone! When Prince Albert, only twenty years after the death of George IV, tried to restructure the Palace and to make 'a new east front to the Palace, clear out and rearrange rooms in the south wing, make alterations in the north wing, new kitchen and offices with ballroom over, take down the Marble Arch, redecorate, paint and alter the drains', he asked for a mere £150,000 from the public purse.* The humorous periodical *Punch* depicted Prince Albert addressing an audience of the London poor. 'Such is our distress,' he pleads, 'that we should be truly grateful for the blessing of a comfortable two-pair back, with commonly decent sleeping-rooms for our children

---

*Bruce Graeme, *The Story of Buckingham Palace* (1928) p.250.

and domestics.' Class envy and money envy are not new in Britain.

Nevertheless, while the British people have always resented giving any money to their Sovereigns, the degree of rancour and envy which has crept into the discussion of Queen Elizabeth II's finances has become ugly to behold. For that reason I do not want this to be a long chapter, even though its subject – money – might turn out to be the one single factor which brings about the fall of the House of Windsor.

Throughout 1992, the calls for the Queen to pay income tax became increasingly strident, and it was in the summer of that year, while the Prime Minister was staying with her at Balmoral, that she confided in him her decision that she *should* pay tax. They agreed to delay an announcement of this until the scandals about the Royal marriages had died down, possibly until the Spring Budget of 1993. Then came the Windsor Fire, with the disclosure that none of the Royal palaces is insured, and that Governments undertake to pay for their refurbishment and upkeep. The idea that the bill for repairing the damage at Windsor might cost the taxpayer £60 million, at a time of profound recession and high unemployment, could not have been more unfortunate from the royalist point of view. In the event, to allay further speculation about the matter and to quieten the critics, the announcement was made in February 1993 that the Queen would pay tax.

The *Daily Mirror* on February 12 carried a full-length cartoon on the front page, depicting the Queen in a tiara and a row of pearls staring avariciously at a pocket calculator. The headline was H. M. THE TAX DODGER. It was the cruellest picture of the Queen ever to be printed outside the underworld of 'satirical' journalism. Rather than welcoming the fact that the Queen was to pay some tax, the paper took an abrasive line. 'The Queen's astonishing tax "dodge" was branded an insult to the ordinary punter last night' – by whom? By some 'sub' on the *Daily Mirror*, presumably. 'Top accountants' – two telephone calls to friends in accountants firms? – 'said nobody else could wriggle out of paying tax on so many perks. And MPs protested the whole deal stank of one law for the rich and another for the poor. Under the "save as you reign" arrangement, the Queen won't pay inheritance tax.' Presumably not, since when her heirs inherit she will be dead, but go on. 'Nor will she pay tax on her palaces, her art collection, jewels, and private use of the yacht *Britannia*, royal flights and royal trains . . .' And so on.

The radio in Britain that morning seemed obsessed by the royal train, and Parliamentarians, full of reforming zeal, who claimed that such 'luxuries' as a royal train or the royal yacht could no longer be supplied by the taxpayer and it was time to 'streamline the monarchy', get rid of the State coaches, reduce the staff at Buckingham Palace and Clarence House, or wear slightly cheaper crowns at a cut-price Coronation ceremony.

Rather than weary the reader with details and statistics, I should like to discuss the essential principles by which decisions could be reached concerning the wealth of the House of Windsor.

First, let us be clear that whether or not she is the richest woman in the world, as is sometimes claimed, or the fourteenth richest (as I saw claimed in a newspaper recently), the Queen is a very rich woman. Since Great Britain has an hereditary Monarchy, I fail to see how any distinction can be made between her public and her private wealth. The only category of person to whom she could be compared in Britain is the higher rank of aristocrat – figures like the Dukes of Devonshire and Buccleuch, who own vast estates, great houses, huge art collections. Ownership in these contexts becomes a notion different in kind from the ownership by a bourgeois of his house, car and portfolio of investments. In an egalitarian society, wealth on a ducal scale might provoke gasps of envy. Many of us would like to be as 'rich' as the Duke of Westminster – said to be the richest man in England – or the Duke of Devonshire. But there is a sense in which these immensely wealthy Dukes, as well as being affluent individuals, are almost in the nature of being institutions. It would be extremely difficult for them to cash in all their 'wealth', and even if they did so – if, for example, the Duke of Devonshire sold Chatsworth and Bolton Abbey and Eastbourne and the Burlington Arcade in London and all his other 'possessions', and went to live in Palm Beach with a bank account worth several billion dollars – these vast chunks of real estate would still need to be 'owned' and administered by some other person or body. If such a thing were to happen, 'the taxpayer' would be no better off. On the whole – there are exceptions – the Dukes have been good landlords, and experiments in the public 'ownership' of land or of great houses do not suggest that committees or government departments or private bodies such as the National Trust make better or more responsible custodians of paintings, houses, forests or coastlines than do individuals and families.

The Queen's 'wealth' is, like the wealth of Dukes, huge. If the Monarchy were abolished and she were allowed to keep, say, Sandringham, Balmoral and the private investments in her portfolio, she would be a very rich private individual. But, of course, she has no intention of abandoning the Monarchy, and it is fanciful to make these distinctions. Since she embodies in her own person the institution of the Monarchy, and since she is the Head of State, she is the custodian, for her lifetime, not merely of Balmoral and

Sandringham and two studs of racehorses and a roomful of jewels – but also of Windsor Castle, Buckingham Palace and all the other, now disused, Royal palaces, such as Hampton Court and the Tower of London. She also 'owns' the State coaches, the royal yacht, the royal train and the royal parks in London. In so far as she is the Head of State, there is a sort of absurdity about her having to pay tax to herself. It is often pointed out that earlier Monarchs paid income tax, but this was in the days when income tax was a penny or little more in the pound, and because they did so it does not mean that they were right to do so.

The reasons given for Queen Elizabeth II paying tax are purely cosmetic. Politicians wish to see her as an immensely rich woman who is not 'contributing' to an expensive Welfare State of Parliament's devising. Before her decision to pay tax on a regular basis, she was in fact making a substantial contribution to State revenues from her income from the Duchy of Lancaster, just as Prince Charles, before the new arrangements came into force, used to pay to the Inland Revenue a considerable portion of his income from the Duchy of Cornwall.

Any rich landowner of even remotely comparable substance could not survive in modern Britain, with its confiscatory levels of taxation and its punitive inheritance tax, without all sorts of clever arrangements, which the *Daily Mirror* would call tax dodges. Without such arrangements, however, there would be no 'stately homes' in private ownership, and all houses like Chatsworth, and most of the English countryside, would be in the hands of public bodies. If one wants to see what this would be like, one only has to visit those parts of Scotland formerly in private ownership and now handed over to the Forestry Commission. All the great estates in England would be a forest of

Christmas trees within a generation without some form of 'tax dodging' by their landlords.

Most landlords and rich men, however – that is, the very rich, but not those in the Duke of Devonshire league – will be paying less tax than the Queen for the simple reason that they do not pay tax at all. Levels of taxation in Britain are so high that the huge majority of the rich long ago put all their wealth 'offshore' and tied up their houses, furniture, paintings and properties in a variety of 'dodges' which keep them safe for their heirs. One can imagine how the *Daily Mirror* and Mr Hattersley would respond if the Queen behaved like a real 'tax dodger' – making her mother into a registered charity or placing the bulk of her loose cash in offshore securities. In the sudden demand for the Queen to pay tax, she is being victimised in a way which no other great landowner or art-collector would find tolerable. For example, any other great landowner who found himself faced with a huge tax bill would feel himself entitled to raise the revenue by charging entry to all his properties. Tourists at the moment have to pay to visit the Queen's Picture Gallery in London, the Tower of London and Windsor Castle and Hampton Court. It would be interesting to see the public reaction if the Queen charged motorists a toll every time they drove through Regent's Park or charged dog-owners for walking Fido in Kensington Gardens. Advocates of taxing the Queen would probably say that these Royal Parks (which were not always open to the public) are now 'public property'. But the same people would have no difficulty in describing a State coach or a royal train – only used for the purpose of serving or entertaining the public – as a 'tax perk'.

So it is necessary to 'clear the mind of cant', as Dr Johnson would say, before discussing the question of Royal money; and it is also necessary to clear the mind of distaste, either for the greed of individual members of the Royal House or for the vulgar envy of wealth in any form which is part of the British character.

The Queen's income derives from four main sources. The first – the most obvious 'drain on the taxpayer' – is the Civil List, which was last fixed in 1990. This grants Her Majesty £7.9 million a year for her official expenditure. Seventy per cent of this is devoted to the (usually quite modest) salaries of those who work directly for the Queen in her official capacity: those, in fact, whom any Head of State would have to employ, whether she were a Queen or an elected President: secretaries, clerical workers, civil servants who help with the State papers, organisers of public engagements, meetings and functions. There are also entertainment expenses which would probably be as great, if not greater, whoever were the Head of State – such things as garden parties. The Queen entertains over 40,000 people each year. Her stationery bill is £139,000 each year, and in 1990 she spent £123,000 on computers. One might consider this an absurd waste of money, but it needs to be seen in context. The computers on almost every British Rail platform announcing from a barely readable screen the times of train arrivals and departures cost £20,000 each – there must be thousands of them in Britain. Any large corporation or company would consider the Queen's expenditure on computers as modest, though one must observe that the Monarchy got on perfectly well without computers for hundreds of years.

If a surge of public opinion led to the collapse of the Monarchy and the election of Mr Roy Hattersley as President, it is doubtful whether he would be able to manage on as little as £7.9 million from the Civil List. Doubtless, he would try to cut down here and there, and have fewer footmen – perhaps even fewer computers. But then he would still need secretaries and paper and envelopes, and presumably, even in the austere rule of President Hattersley, there would be the occasional Presidential garden party or State banquet.

The second source of the Queen's income is the Grant in Aid, and this is the area which is most likely to be attacked by the reforming politicians. These are annual funds which are granted by Parliament for the upkeep of the Royal Palaces and those 'grace and favour' residences given to the Queen's family, favourites or servants of high or low degree: Buckingham Palace, St James's Palace, Clarence House, Marlborough House, the residential office and the general areas of Kensington Palace, Frogmore House and Hampton Court Mews and Paddocks. The Royal Palaces Agency looks after the unoccupied palaces. Three-quarters of the money for these buildings is spent on maintenance. It is again hard to see how the sum would be reduced in the event of President Hattersley taking control. If these buildings, nearly all of them of great historic interest, were to be maintained, it would still cost the same to maintain them whether there were a Queen or not.

The debatable area here is how much the Queen should be expected to make a contribution from her other areas of income towards the maintenance of her palaces. Had the question of her paying tax never arisen, this might have seemed perfectly reasonable. Why should not one part of the Queen's income – whether you call it 'private' or not – be used to finance her houses? But as soon as the Government has said that it regards some of her wealth as 'private', then there seems no reason why she should dip into this to pay for essentially 'public works', like the restoration of the State Banqueting Hall at Windsor: is anyone pretending that if she were a private individual she would have State Banquets? And if it is conceded that the restoration at Windsor is a public work, then it surely falls into the same category as the building of roads or the repair of any other public monument. We should not ask the Queen, merely because she is very rich, to pay for Nelson's Column if it fell down. No doubt, however, the Parliamentarians and the newspapers will want to have things both ways and claim that the Queen ought to pay for Windsor because she lives there. But this is a circular argument which could go on for ever. She lives there not because she is a plutocrat who got out her cheque-book one day and decided she would like to buy a luxurious castle within easy reach of Heathrow. Airport. She lives there because she is Queen. The reformers are in danger of persecuting Elizabeth Windsor as an individual because of their muddled ideas of the monarchical function.

The third source of the Queen's income comes from revenue designated by the Privy Purse. Nearly all of this comes from the Duchy of Lancaster; a much smaller part comes from estate revenue from Sandringham. In the year 1992 the net surplus was £3.6 million, most of it from rents. The Privy Purse pays for the estate workers at Sandringham and those who administer the Duchy of Lancaster, which owns 11,800 acres of Staffordshire, Cheshire and Shropshire; 10,700 acres in the Fylde and Forest of Bowland; 8,000 acres of Yorkshire near Scarborough, and 3,000 acres in Northamptonshire and Lincolnshire. These estates are administered in the same way as the estates owned by Oxford and Cambridge Colleges, or by the Duchy of Cornwall, or by the great landowners like the Duke of Westminster. There is no evidence that the Queen creams off crippling profits from the Duchy of Lancaster. If it is proposed by the reformers that the Duchy of Lancaster be administered by the Government, the saving to the taxpayer would be the equivalent of what was wasted in approximately two minutes on 'Black Wednesday', when the Treasury was vainly trying to defend the value of the pound sterling before its ignominious retreat from the ERM.

These, then, are the three chief areas of the Queen's income. And what the Hattersleys are slow to recognise is that almost none of this money would be saved if the Queen were to be replaced by an elected President. We should still need someone to clean the windows at Buckingham Palace, whether it was the Queen's face or President Hattersley's looking out of them. It must also be said that, compared with some of the other things on which the politicians are prepared to spend the taxpayers' money, the Monarchy is not ludicrously expensive.

The fourth area of the Queen's income is what is known as her personal wealth – such things as her investment portfolio and her private income. No other taxpayer is obliged to disclose their annual income, but this does not stop even the more respectable newspapers speculating about the Queen's private wealth and imagining how much or how little she will have to pay to the Inland Revenue. I have already intimated my own view, that it is difficult to distinguish between what is owned by the Queen as an individual and what is owned by her as Head of State. To have made the distinction implies, on her part, a lack of confidence that the House of Windsor will go on forever. It seems like the equivalent of a packed suitcase or a foreign bank account. As such, her ill-advised decision to pay tax has weakened the Monarchy.

The reformers who pine to make the British Monarchy more like the simple, bicycling monarchies of Northern Europe have been vociferous lately in expressing their wish that much of the ostentation and ceremony of the Monarchy be reduced. I began this chapter with some harsh words about the personal greed and ostentation of some members of the Royal Family – a fact which, in prosperous times, the British people have overlooked, but which in times of hardship will make them hated. But I should not like to end this discussion of Royal money on a carping or a cheese-paring note. Of all the most ridiculous suggestions which I have heard in the endless discussions of these matters on television and radio, the prize for the most absurd must go to the Member of Parliament who felt it would be 'appropriate' for the Queen to get rid of the State coach and to travel to the Palace of Westminster in a car. The one aspect of Royal life to which only the most dogged killjoys would object is its pageantry. The Queen owns a great number of coaches: let her ride in them. No photograph ever taken of her in private life suggests that she is the sort of person who would be remotely tempted to wear ostentatious jewels at home. She is not the Duchess of Windsor. Tweeds and twinsets and headscarves are her style at Sandringham and Balmoral. But when she is in London opening Parliament, please do not let us have her doing it on her bicycle. We want crown, robes and State coaches. When she entertains visiting Heads of State and gives them a banquet, as she owns tiaras by the score: let her wear them. Her cupboards are groaning with gold plates, bought by George IV. It costs us nothing for her to have them laid on her table. What possible service will have been performed to anyone by putting these things in a museum and never using them? Though the Royal Family, like all rich people, excite envy when they flaunt their wealth, they are also unlike any other wealthy people. When she wears the crown, the Queen reminds us that the crown itself is greater than the head that wears it. George V used to wear a crown each day while signing State papers, to remind himself of this fact. Very odd it must have looked, with his pepper-and-salt Norfolk jacket and his plus-fours.

This matter of the Royal money will not, of course, die down. Motivated by muddle and malice, the politicians and the journalists will go on and on carping, and the Queen, as she always does, will bow to their requests and demands. 'Anything to please': that was the phrase that Edward VIII kept repeating. Only, now she has made the first concession and chosen to pay tax, nothing will please. It will be a sad day when they persuade her to put all her jewels and all her coaches in a museum, for the Royal pageantry is very much the best part of the Royal act, and certainly the most popular. There are few finer spectacles in the world than the Queen in her uniform taking part in the ceremony of Trooping the Colour, or the Queen in her robes of State processing through the House of Lords at Westminster to open Parliament. Inappropriate, though, as Hattersley would want to remind us, for the last decade of the twentieth century. Highly inappropriate in John Major's 'classless society'.

ELEVEN

A Modest Proposal

My friends, it is not good to be without a servant
in this world; but to be without master, it appears,
is a still fataler predicament for some.

Thomas Carlyle, *Essays*

Let us rehearse very briefly the position of the British
Monarchy today. We find an ancient, much-valued institution under violent assault from the Press for very largely
frivolous reasons (some Punch-and-Judy marital quarrels, a
'dirty' telephone call). In a time of recession and economic
hardship, the personal wealth of the Windsors has awoken
a particularly nasty outbreak of money-envy, a disease
endemic in Britain.

But we have also seen that there are serious causes
for concern that the House of Windsor is no longer
in a position to fulfil the traditional functions of constitutional kingship. We have taken those functions to
fall under three general headings. The Monarch is the
Defender of the Faith and the upholder of the Church
of England. This position has been made very difficult
for the present Queen, not because of anything which
has happened to her or her family, but because the

religious 'map' of Britain has changed radically since her accession. The clergy might quarrel about the exact numbers whom it is possible to describe as 'practising Anglicans', but it seems beyond doubt that only a tiny proportion of the Queen's subjects are practising members of her Church, compared with the high proportion who are religiously indifferent, and the significant number of Muslims, Hindus, Sikhs and Roman Catholics. Given this change in Britain since 1953, and given the changes in relations between the Christian Churches and the growth of the ecumenical movement, it is no longer deemed suitable by the Church of England itself and by its two primates, the Archbishops of Canterbury and York, to ask any new Sovereign to swear an oath at the Coronation to uphold the Protestant religion. The Church of England has itself changed, and the schism following the Synod's decision to authorise the ordination of women to the priesthood makes it all the harder to speak of Anglicanism as the official or the given, still less the Established, religion of England.

If all these difficulties would face Elizabeth II, a devout woman in good standing with her Church, what difficulties would be added were she to be succeeded by Prince Charles! His marital status would make it extremely hard for him to become the Supreme Governor of a Church which still forbids divorce. And it now looks certain that he and his wife will be divorced. It was the impossibility of Edward VIII marrying a divorced woman which forced him to renounce the throne. If the House of Windsor is true to its own rule of life, it is hard to see how Prince Charles could claim to be the Defender of the Faith. The difficulty caused by his marital status is this: if or when the Coronation Oath is changed (for the reasons which we have discussed), it would *look* as if the Church were fudging its principles in order to accommodate Prince Charles. Either way he cannot win, whether the Church and State alter their relations or remain the same. The Evangelical wing of the Church of England have said that they would not be able to support the Church if the Protestant Promise were removed from the Coronation Service; nor, say they, would they be able to accept an apparent adulterer as the Supreme Governor of the Church, though this stringent proviso, it must be said, would have eliminated all previous Defenders of the Faith from being crowned, with the possible exceptions of Charles I, George III, Queen Victoria and George VI.

It would seem, then, as though the House of Windsor has reached a crossroads over the religious question. Either it abandons its own religious 'Windsor rules', those rules which led to the destruction of Edward VIII and the Coronation of the virtuous George VI, or it vetoes Charles III.

The second great function of the British Royal Family has been to serve as figureheads of happy family life. Prince Albert laid particular stress on this, which was why the libertine behaviour of his eldest son Bertie caused him such heartbreak. George V and George VI were both in their slightly different ways puritans in the Prince Albert mould. Queen Elizabeth emphasised the differences between her own wholesome, aristocratic friends and the 'fast set' favoured by Edward VIII. The Little Princesses were the very types and embodiments of wholesomeness. And it was a similar image of family life which the present Queen was encouraged to display in her television film *Royal Family*. It could be argued here, as in the case of the specific question of religion, that the world had changed since 1953. In those days, when divorced persons were not allowed in the Royal Enclosure at Ascot, it would not have been thinkable that all the immediate Royal Family who had attempted marriage would have failed in it: Princess Margaret, divorced; Princess Anne divorced and remarried; Prince Andrew, soon to be divorced; Prince Charles, on the road to divorce and legally separated. Attitudes to sexual morality in Royal circles have now relaxed to the point where homosexuals may now bring their partners to Buckingham Palace garden parties. Considering the loyal service given to all the Royal Households by homosexuals, this is nothing more than justice.*

In these circumstances, as we have suggested, it might be said that with its high incidence of divorce and its smattering of homosexuality, the Royal Family are now a more representative figurehead to a nation where there are so many broken homes and where there is a high incidence of homosexuality. It is doubtful whether King George V and Queen Mary would have seen things in quite this way. Once again it would seem as if the House of Windsor were faced with a choice: either it abandons 'Windsor Rules' or it abandons Prince Charles – and, indeed, all the Queen's children. Many people would find it extremely distressing that the Royal Family had cynically relinquished its claim to represent 'family values' just so that it could hold tenaciously to the Crown.

The third function of Monarchy which we have examined in this book is its constitutional role in the narrowly political sense. Bagehot saw the Sovereign's role as 'to be consulted, to encourage, and occasionally to warn'. For

* For obvious reasons, the unmarried make happier Royal servants than the married since Kings, Queens and Princes tend to be so demanding. The story of the Queen Mother's telephone call to her butler's pantry, while she sat impatiently in her drawing-room, can bear repetition: 'I don't know about you old queens, but this Old Queen wants a drink.'

this system to work, it presupposes a willingness by the Prime Minister to acknowledge the Sovereign's traditional place in the scheme of things, and we suggested that it was in part Margaret Thatcher's abrasive attitude to the Queen which helped to precipitate the present difficulty.

But since Prince Charles is still the heir to the throne, we must ask whether his career to date inspires confidence. When asked how he had learned his role, Prince Charles once replied, 'As monkeys learn, by watching their mothers.' One can only conclude, a little sadly, that he has not watched his mother carefully enough. There is only one occasion – her disagreement with Mrs Thatcher over South Africa – in his mother's reign where she was seen openly to clash with her Prime Minister. In the case of Prince Charles and the GATT talks, it was he who shot his mouth off with potentially calamitous results, not merely for his country but for the world. Deprived of any real function, Prince Charles would appear to relish the headline-grabbing potential of adopting 'controversial' attitudes, and this could be of the greatest possible danger in the years ahead, particularly if, as we argued in Chapter Nine, the Monarchy is moving into a phase where it is more politically necessary, and where the situation in Britain (poised between Island Fortress Nationalists and Federalist Fanatics) is much more sensitive than it has been for decades. There never was a time when a potential Monarch more needed to imitate the examples of George V and Elizabeth II, for there could so easily come a time when they need to do slightly more than encouraging or warning the politicians. The Royal Prerogative is still potentially a real political power. Only a very experienced or a very wise Monarch will know how to prevent a Prime Minister from abusing this Prerogative to sidestep the wishes of an elected House of Commons or the interests of the British people.

We seem to have reached the position of saying that the British people and the House of Windsor have a choice. Either they choose to continue the monarchical system (with the necessary emendations to the religious part of the Coronation Oath), that system which has been held in trust by the House of Saxe-Coburg since 1837 (renamed Windsor in 1917); or they abandon the 'Windsor Rules' and have a new sort of Monarchy with Prince Charles at the head of it – with no Established Church, no sense of the Monarch as a family emblem, and his only function being political – with the possibility of a future punctuated by policy clashes between the Head of State and the Prime Minister, as happens from time to time in France. It would not be long, if we had such a system, before people began to ask why – since the Monarch's only function seemed to be political – we could not elect a President.

This is a dilemma indeed. It is not an invented problem. It will not go away so long as Prince Charles remains the heir to the throne. But Constitutional Monarchy is by its nature conservative. Its strength is that it provides continuity with the past which could never be offered by recurrent Presidential elections. Not only is it useful to have a Head of State (as the British do now) with a long political memory stretching back to the time of Churchill; it is appreciated on the deepest level by the people that, in an ever-changing world, the Monarchy should remain the same because the persons of the Royal Family also remain the same.

The British Monarchy is seen at its best on ceremonial occasions. During the *annus horribilis* of 1992 we might have forgotten this, because it probably seemed as though we never saw a Royal personage in a newspaper unless they were committing adultery or conducting a lawsuit

or making some crassly foolish speech about the way
the rest of us should live. But, even during that year,
Trooping the Colour took place on Horseguards Parade
in June: the Queen in her uniform reviewed her brightly
arrayed troops, providing something infinitely more than a
pageant, an important national ritual which linked together
tribal feelings of belonging, ideas of the past and feelings of
intense loyalty. At the Cenotaph in November, the Sovereign is the first person to lay a wreath in memory of those
who died in the World Wars. Once again it is of immense
symbolic significance that it should be a Monarch who does
this, rather than some politician. Of course, politicans are
there, and the heavens would not fall if politicians alone
attended the ceremony; but most of the old airmen and
soldiers and sailors would say that they wanted to see
the Queen there. The Monarch is able at such moments
to stand for a whole nation, not because of her character
or her 'qualifications' but purely by virtue of the fact that
she is the Queen.

It is on such occasions of national mourning or rejoicing
that one sees the point of having a Monarch who is a
'figurehead'. Nations have these feelings, whether or not
sophisticated people might smile at or mock them. They are
most easily focused on individuals. One wonders whether
the history of Germany might not have been different in the
1930s had the Kaiser not been forced to live in exile. When,
today, one objects to the garish or immoral behaviour of
the younger members of the Royal Family, it is less on puritanical than on constitutional grounds. The best constitutional Monarch would be one, like Queen Elizabeth II, who
was, in all public senses of the word, slightly colourless,
and who had the humility and the dullness of nature not
to draw attention to herself. It would be a figure whom the
country at large might plausibly reverence as Sovereign,

but not a 'personality' whom the people should be asked to admire as if she were a politician or a film actress; it should perhaps be someone like the present Queen, about whom not very much (in the last resort) is really known.

The misbehaviour and misfortunes of the young Windsors provide amusing copy for newspapers, but the best sort of royalties would be the sort of people whose lives were so blameless and so discreet and so dull that we never really wanted to read about them unless we were addicted to reading the Court Circular. If Prince Charles were to become King in the near future, it is not difficult to imagine the response of the Press. Hardly a month would pass without a story of one of his alleged mistresses; and this would provoke his wife, or ex-wife as she would be by then, into newer frenzies of self-advertisement. A fine way for the young Princes, and in particular the Heir Presumptive, Prince William, to grow up and be prepared for the office of Monarchy!

It might well finish off the British Monarchy if Prince Charles were to attempt such a 'bumpy ride'. Institutions can only survive if they can be demonstrated to have a function within the real world and Prince Charles's position and personal history sadly disqualify him from embodying those values and exercising those duties which were so faithfully fulfilled by the three great Windsor Monarchs – George V, George VI and Elizabeth II.

The solution proposed in the Press by the Princess's party, as it came to be known, was that Prince Charles should stand down in favour of his son, and that his wife should, in the event of the Queen dying before Prince William reached his majority, be Princess Regent. The Princess's party was not, as some people supposed, governed by a childishly besotted love of Lady Di; it was attempting to find a serious answer to the crisis in the House of Windsor. It grieves me to write these words, as a stalwart of the Princess's party, but Lady Di no longer looks like a plausible Princess Regent. Her disloyalty to the Royal Family, her hysterical nature, her indiscretion with journalists and her ludicrous friends really make the prospect of her being a suitable guardian of the constitutional Monarchy seem wholly implausible.

The House of Windsor, one must recognise this, has reached the end of the road. One should not be surprised. If one counts their tenure of the throne as dating from 1837, then they have been serving their country for close on 160 years. The Tudors, the last great dynasty of comparable longevity, lasted 126 years, and the Hanoverians 123 years. There is every reason for thinking that, while the Monarchy should continue, it could benefit from a new dynasty, or at least from a different one. The disadvantage of this idea, of course, is that one of the great strengths of an hereditary Monarchy should be the continuity which it provides with the nation's past. Merely to shove in, arbitrarily, some other family and put a crown on the head of its most eligible male would be to institute a presidency or a dictatorship in kingly regalia. This would be Bonapartism not Monarchism.

What Britain needs is an ancient Monarchy with strong family links to the House of Windsor; and what the Monarchy needs is a release from the impossible prospect of King Charles III, or Queen Anne Laurence, or King Andrew, separated from Queen Fergie and her daughters. If we were right to suppose that the ideal constitutional Monarch would be of a quiet disposition, uninterested in the allure of 'fame' and bored by the prospect of 'stardom', then the Princess Regent, however much we may love her, seems equally unsuitable for the role.

As it happens, a solution is to hand.

If we consult the history books, we discover that the claims of both the Stuarts and the Hanoverians to the

English throne from the late-seventeenth century onwards were in the highest degree questionable. On April 9, 1649, barely two months after the execution of Charles I, a son was born in Rotterdam to Charles II and one Lucy Walter. Both the parents were under twenty years of age – after a rackety career, Lucy was to die in Paris, in 1658, of 'a disease incidental to her manner of living'; the aspersion is that of James II, Charles II's brother. James, who inherited the Crown from his brother, had every reason to cast as many slurs as possible upon Lucy Walter and her son, the Duke of Monmouth. Certainly, as early as 1662 Pepys had heard the rumour that Charles II intended to make the Duke of Monmouth his legitimate heir. The King doted upon his son, heaped honours upon him and allowed him to bear the Royal Arms. It was said that the King and Lucy Walter had been married, which would have meant that the Duke of Monmouth was in fact the legitimate heir to the English Crown. The rebellion of Monmouth and his Protestant supporters against the Catholic James II was not successful. The matter was settled after Charles's death by the Battle of Sedgemoor, the last battle ever fought on English soil, on July 5, 1685. Having lost this battle, Monmouth was brought to London to be beheaded. The axeman bungled his work. According to one eyewitness, he struck the Duke five blows and 'severed not his head from his body till he cut it off with his knife'. According to the entry for the Duke of Monmouth in the *Dictionary of National Biography*, 'not a tittle of real evidence exists in favour of the supposed marriage between Charles II and Lucy Walter', but Monmouth always maintained that he possessed the proof of his legitimacy. The marriage certificate of Lucy and Charles II was said to be contained in a black box entrusted by Bishop Cosin of Durham to his son-in-law Sir Gilbert Gerard. It was claimed that Lucy Walter had been a penitent of

Cosin's when he was living in Paris before the Restoration.

Years later, when Queen Victoria was on the throne, it is said that the Duke of Buccleuch, the heir and descendant of Monmouth, produced this marriage certificate and showed it to his Sovereign. Then, as a gesture of his loyalty to the House of Saxe-Coburg, he tossed it into his grate and burnt it in front of the Queen.

It might have been more prudent had he kept it, for this would have enabled the whole question of Monmouth's legitimacy, and his claim to the English throne, to be rehearsed all over again. In an article in the *Spectator*,* the magazine's deputy editor Simon Courtauld put forward the case for maintaining the Monarchy and disposing of the services of the House of Windsor. Having recognised the unsuitability of Jacobite claimants to the English throne, such as Albrecht, Duke of Bavaria,† who at eighty-seven might be thought a little old to make a lively contender, Mr Courtauld resurrects the Monmouth claim and suggests that on the Queen's death the Crown should pass to the Dukes of Buccleuch.

'The Buccleuchs', he writes, 'would now be admirably suited to succeed to the British throne. The present Duke ... is a larger landowner than the Queen. If the Windsors wanted to hang on to their rather dreary piles at Sandringham and Balmoral, the Buccleuchs are happily seated at Dalkeith Palace near Edinburgh, Bowhill in Selkirk, Drumlanrig Castle in Dumfriess & Galloway and Boughton in Northamptonshire – where they have one of the finest art collections in Europe. When the time comes, they should be ready to step into the breach.'

*January 2, 1993.
†The Duke is descended, through the House of Savoy, from Henrietta, Duchess of Orleans, sister of Charles II and daughter of Charles I.

The Courtauld scheme is very nearly, but not quite, the right answer. The drawback is its oddness. The public, unaware of the story of the Duke of Monmouth and probably largely unaware of the Duke of Buccleuch, would feel that someone was trying to pull a fast one. There would be a 'Hands off our Charlie' movement if you tried to persuade people that the King's residence was Bowhill, not Buckingham Palace. Courtauld's sympathies are too aristocratic.

But all good Monarchists owe him a debt of gratitude for reviving the Monmouth claim, since it points us in the right direction. The reader will remember that what we are looking for is someone to carry on the Monarchy in the honest, dull tradition of George V, George VI and Queen Elizabeth II. We are looking for someone who is not a vulgarian whose wife likes posing for the television cameras, but is a decent, quiet sort, preferably someone in whom it would be impossible to take very much interest, even if we tried. We are looking for a man or woman who would provide some continuity with the Royal past, but who would also draw a firm *finis* upon the claims of the poor Queen's unsuitable children to inherit the throne. Ideally, therefore, we should be looking for someone who is descended both from King George V and – to satisfy the Monmouth legitimists – from the Dukes of Buccleuch.

Such a man there is: Richard, Duke of Gloucester. It is true that some of the Duke's known opinions – such as that Richard III did not kill the Princes in the Tower, or that cigarettes are bad for your health – suggest that he is not a person of complete common sense. But we are looking for a constitutional Monarch, not a paragon. His father, Henry, Duke of Gloucester, was the fourth child of George V and Queen Mary. Prince Henry was an unsophisticated man with an endearing weakness for the bottle. For much of his life he was a professional soldier. His heir, the present

Duke's brother William, was sadly killed in an air crash in 1972. Prince Richard, who had never expected to inherit the Dukedom, trained as an architect, but since he became Duke has largely devoted himself to running the family estates at Barnwell in Northamptonshire. He is married to an attractive Dane, Birgitte van Deurs, and they have three fine children. His mother, Princess Alice, believes them to be pitiably poor – 'they cannot afford a chauffeur, a lady's maid or a valet'.* It is the same Princess Alice, of course, who provides the Duke with his Monmouth connection, since she was the third daughter of the seventh Duke of Buccleuch.

For the Queen to declare that the Duke of Gloucester and all his legitimate descendants were henceforth to be the heirs to the British Crown would certainly be better than doing nothing, if she wishes to guarantee the future of the Monarchy. That she would ever make such a declaration is, unfortunately, unlikely; and that the mild-mannered bespectacled Duke would himself, like his ancestor Monmouth, take up arms to assert his right to the throne is even less likely. Anyone who hopes that the Monarchy has a future must await the Queen's demise with some trepidation and hope that it is a long time off. What this book has tried to show is that it is not so much a question of whether Prince Charles would make a passable King or a good King, but whether – as that role is at present defined – he could possibly be King at all. And once an heir to the throne is seen to be ineligible, it becomes inevitable that there will be talk of a republic.

In Britain in the last forty years many good, old things have passed away, less because there was widespread enthusiasm for the new than that there was not sufficiently

*Kenneth Rose, *Kings, Queens and Courtiers* (1985) p. 136.

articulate expression by the mass of people in defence of the old. Prince Charles, about whom some harsh things have been said in this book, surely deserves praise for his attempt, since a famous speech in 1984, to speak up for what the huge majority of people have felt about the modernistic style in architecture. Only a handful of architects and aesthetic fanatics ever liked the modern style, and most city-dwellers in Europe hate what this style has done to their cities. And yet nearly all the towns in England were spoilt during the 1960s, because everyone took the old style for granted and so few people voiced any protest at the wreckage. A comparable thing happened in the Church. Few people except cranks could have preferred the hideous modern liturgies to the ancient time-honoured words of the old. Certainly in the English Church, the *Book of Common Prayer* and the Authorised Version of the Bible were cast aside almost without discussion. Wherever one went in England, anguish was expressed about this, but the anguish got nobody anywhere. It seemed slightly 'cranky' to join any society or action group to save the old Prayer Book.

The English have a fear of seeming odd by sticking their necks out and complaining at change. They will grumble quietly among themselves when changes have taken place and agree that they were changes for the worse, but it is seldom that they will take action before a change has become irrevocable and say that it is not a change which they want. It is this indifferentism in the English which is the republicans' strongest weapon. A republican newspaper proprietor, Rupert Murdoch, has made it quite clear that he intends to continue to fill his newspapers, especially the vulgar ones like the *Sun* and the *Sunday Times*, with as much filth as he can muster about the House of Windsor. Any sexual indiscretion they might commit will find its way on to Murdoch's front pages. Nor will his editors miss any chance to attack the wealth and privilege and position of the Monarchy, so that matters will reach the point when the Parliamentarians can say that there is now a 'popular' groundswell against the Monarchy itself. When they attack the Queen, her defenders can say that these attacks are contemptible, since she is peerless and as nearly perfect as it is possible for a constitutional Monarch to be. It is a very different matter when they attack the Queen's children, or when those children themselves use the newspapers to attack one another. It looks perilously as if the Monarchy is going to be one of those things, like the architecture of the older English cities and the language of the old English Church, which is simply allowed to go because no one can think of a good word to save it.

When it has gone, there will be grumbling. More than the House of Windsor will fall if the Monarchy is allowed to be hounded out by bullies and brutes. It will be a symptom of the general coarsening of life in Britain today, in which the brashly new inevitably defeats the old, in which the ugly always overcomes the beautiful, and everything of which the British used to be proud is cast down and vilified. It is too much to hope in modern Britain – filthy, chaotic, idle, rancorous modern Britain – that sweetness and light could ever triumph over barbarism. The Queen is the only individual in British public life who has held out some hope that decency might survive. By failing the trust which she put in them, her children have failed us all. The lights have not quite gone out. But they are guttering in their sockets.

Epilogue

On Friday, January 14, 1994, the Duchess of Kent, a figure too good, too innocent, and too private to have played any part in the previous pages of this book, was received into the Roman Catholic Church. She was the first member of the British Royal Family to become Catholic since King James II in the seventeenth century. True, the likelihood of the Duchess ever becoming Queen of England in the future is very remote. Her husband, the Duke of Kent, is a cousin of Queen Elizabeth II, and is eighteenth in line to the throne. It would take an extremely enterprising airborne contingent of the Irish Republican Army, bombarding, let us say, the Royal Family Christmas at Sandringham, before the Duke of Kent came anywhere near becoming a king.

The Duchess's decision, however, has a symbolic significance. No one doubts her deep personal piety.* She has never made any secret of her Anglo Catholic affinities,

---

*Vide, The House of Windsor and the Church, p. 224.

and much of her time has been spent in those High Church shrines, convents, and orphanages which would be least willing to accept the epithet 'protestant'. She was known to share, with her ritualist coreligionists, a profound disquiet about the unilateral decision of the English Church to ordain women to the priesthood, in defiance of a plea from the English Cardinal, Basil Hume, that such a step would damage relations between Canterbury and Rome. Only months before the first woman was ordained, the Duchess joined those many Anglicans who took the Path to Rome.

How does this private journey of faith affect the fortunes of the House of Windsor? And what is its symbolic significance?

To answer the second question first: this conversion destroys the illusion that the Church of England is any more than a minor, and somewhat discredited, sect, whose claim to represent the people of England at prayer seems increasingly impudent. True, the cathedrals, abbeys, and ancient parish churches of England are still administered by functionaries of the Anglican Church. For reasons which are atavistic as well as aesthetic, people continue to marry in these places and to conduct funerals for their dead in them, precisely because they are spots 'whereon the founders lived and died'. But the number of practicing Anglicans, of Anglicans who go to Holy Communion, are rapidly declining. The Duchess of Kent is known to have yearned to be a Catholic for over ten years. An indiscreet Roman prelate told the newspapers that she had approached him more than a decade ago, and only held back from embracing the papal obedience for fear of distressing the Queen. Clearly, after the *annus horribilis*, the Queen felt that one more or less distress would make little difference. She has given the

Duchess, or 'Moonie'* as she calls her in private, her blessing to follow her own conscience. The symbolic effect of the Duchess's decision is to make everyone realize that the Monarchy in England, if it is 'Church of England', is only so definable in the sense that Canterbury Cathedral is 'Church of England' and not as the Archbishop of Canterbury is 'Church of England'. That is to say, the Cathedral is an old building, stained with the blood of a martyr, hallowed with the memories of ten centuries of Englishmen, and part of the warp and woof of national life at a profoundly emotional level. The Archbishop of Canterbury, by contrast, is the representative of a set of beliefs which are shared by only a tiny fraction of his fellow countrymen, and who in all important respects, regardless of his legal status as the third most eminent nobleman in the realm and the Primate of the National Church, is in fact regarded as the deeply unimpressive leader of a spiritually bankrupt sect.

This leads us back to our first point – that the Duchess of Kent's conversion to Catholicism might, paradoxically, be the saving of the House of Windsor. Writing in *The Times*, the former editor of that newspaper, himself a Catholic convert, Lord Rees-Mogg, said this: 'The Act of Settlement would not now stand a determined assault. If Prince Charles wanted to become a Roman Catholic, which he does not, the Government could not enforce the Act of Settlement to prevent him from coming to the throne. Such an act of religious discrimination would contravene the whole spirit of the age'.† This is undoubtedly true, and, in all probability, there will be moves, sooner or later, to repeal the Act of Settlement of 1701, which insists upon the

---

*She received this nickname because of her air of religious gullibility.
†*The Times* (London), January 13, 1994.

Protestant succession, and to repeal at the same time those provisions of the Royal Marriages Act which forbid the Sovereign to marry a Roman Catholic. As soon as the British Parliament has removed the necessity for the Monarch to be a member of the Church of England, it will have removed the *raison d'être* of the Church of England which, after all, only came into being to suit the convenience of the Tudor dynasty. Disestablishment of the Church of England would follow as the night follows day. Few Englishmen or Englishwomen would grieve. The Bishops would be banished from the House of Lords. The Church, which had been brought into being to allow one monarch, Henry VIII, to divorce, would, by its own dissolution, allow another divorced personage, Prince Charles, to become a monarch.

That, certainly, would be the hope of those British monarchists today who wish for a smooth succession from Queen Elizabeth II to King Charles III.

In the year since this book was completed and went to press between hardcovers, Prince Charles and his propagandists have been busy reconstructing his 'image' in the eyes of the press and public. Lest anyone should have supposed that His Royal Highness were a less than perfect parent, there have been a number of tactfully released films of the Prince fondling and ribbing his two sons. Serious newspapers have joined the tabloids in emphasizing the happiness of Prince William and Prince Harry when they spent time with their father, who has continued to show himself a deeply caring man, interested in the environment, architecture, the plight of the urban poor, and the unemployed young. His wife, by contrast, has been represented to the media less and less as a royal personage, and more as a media star. When she has been photographed with her sons, it has been in amusement parks or on exotic foreign beaches, the sort of locations where one might expect to see your favorite actress enjoying herself, rather than a future Queen of England.

When, in November, Diana was photographed exercising in a suburban gymnasium, the pictures were bought, and published, by *The Daily Mirror*. Needless to say, the other newspapers were shocked by this intrusion into her personal privacy. In particular, *The Sunday Times*, which had less than a year earlier published stories about Diana vomiting, and *The Sun*, which had fulfilled its public duty by publishing photographs of a semi-naked Duchess of York dallying with her financial adviser, felt a deep sense of shock at *The Daily Mirror*'s poor behavior. While all the newspapers discussed every aspect of the matter, the Princess of Wales herself felt that she had reached the end of this particular line. She could bear no more. There have been other examples of Royal personages for one reason or another phasing down their public appearances. When the Royal authorities discovered that Diana had tired of her Royal persona and wished to retire from the public stage, they implored her to do so gradually, and in such a way as not to draw attention to herself.

This was tantamount to asking her to do precisely the opposite. As far as Diana was concerned the Royal Family had given her a terrible year. As the months since her separation with Charles unfolded, she had felt increasingly isolated. They removed from her the private detective who had been the trusted friend to both she and her sons. One of her dearest friends, the Brazilian Ambassador to the Court of St. James, was recalled to South America. With her children both at school, Diana was more and more alone. At a charity luncheon at the Dorchester Hotel in November 1993, she astonished the world by announcing, in effect, that she was retiring and that like another mysterious screen-goddess, she wanted to be alone. The announcement was followed, the next day, by an appearance by Diana and Mr. Richard Branson celebrating the triumphs of Virgin Atlantic Airways. So it remains to be seen whether this great diva has actually left the stage, or whether her admirers have seen her merely retreat to the wings for a welcomed respite before the next scene.

The questions which I posed in the foregoing pages, nearly a year ago, have not gone away. If the Queen died tomorrow, there would be considerable confusion. Could the Prince of Wales be crowned Charles III in a religious ceremony in Westminster Abbey and made supreme governor of the Church of England? Could Diana – at the time of this writing, separated from Charles but not divorced – become the Queen of England?

Everyone, of course, hopes that Queen Elizabeth II will not die tomorrow, but she is not immortal, and in spite of all his efforts to rehabilitate himself in the eyes of the British public, Prince Charles still faces major constitutional problems.

If I were to review *The Rise and Fall of the House of Windsor*, I should wish to say two things. One is, that in spite of its occasional moments of weariness and cynicism, its author underestimates the British capacity for humbug and hypocrisy. These, more than anything else, are what will save Prince Charles, and which will probably guarantee that he does, when the sad day dawns, inherit his mother's crown. He will do so, not because he is particularly popular or likeable, or competent, but because most people in Britain (and come to that, most people in the world) wish the British Monarchy to continue. Any number of scandals, and sensational newspaper stories, and denunciations by that dwindling number of clerics who still believe in the Ten

Commandments, will not alter the human craving for kings and kingship.

But though I believe Charles will become king, I think that he, and his subjects, will pay a price. And that price is that no one, not even he, will believe in him. The *annus horribilis* has exposed the House of Windsor, and deprived it of that aura of mystery without which it is not quite possible to put one's trust in kings. It remains to be seen whether, having cast itself loose from the English Church, the House of Windsor will in fact long survive or whether it will discover that, for all its fat, fornicating Hanoverian forebearers, its function in national life was essentially religious. Writing in praise of his new coreligionist, the Duchess of Kent, Lord Rees-Mogg said, 'We can all be grateful to the Duchess of Kent because she is dealing with real questions, and not with what all the religions regard as the superficial illusions of life. The Royal Family is at its strongest when it is seen as the anchor, not of a particular church or sect, but of the religious view of life itself. To that the Duchess of Kent is giving her witness'.*

This is an eloquent testimony, and time will show whether it is plausible, or whether it is no more than a pious hope that, in spite of all its turmoils, the House of Windsor, and with it the British Establishment, the House of Lords, *The Times*, and Lord Rees-Mogg will continue to function in their time-disgraced fashion, with 'business as usual' translating the motives beneath their varied aims and escutcheons. Historians have noted the bonds and links which held the Church of England and the English Crown together. They have drawn our attention to the Scottish Monarchs (the first English King, James) who exclaimed 'No bishop. No king!' And they have noted that in all the

The Times, January 13, 1994.

European countries where religion was overthrown, the Crown was not long to follow. Those who would echo Gabriele d'Annunzio's observation that, 'old legitimate monarchies are everywhere declining, and Demos stands ready to swallow them down its miry throat', have looked on the English scene without surprise. Demos has been able to effect with a telephoto lens and a banner headline what, in less decadent eras of the European story, was achieved by the firing squad and the guillotine.

INDEX

Index

National Portrait Gallery, London 126
National Trust 178
National Union of Mineworkers 16
Neil, Andrew 3–4
New Statesman 71
Nicholas II, Tsar of Russia 9
Nicholson, Harold 90
Norwich, Bishop of 42

Observer 170
One of Us (Young) 25
Orleans, Henrietta, Duchess of 197n
Oxford and Cambridge Colleges 57, 183

Paine, Tom 165
Palmerston, Henry Temple, 3rd Viscount 84
Paris-Match 2, 103
Parker, Michael 131
Parker-Bowles, Andrew 34
Parker-Bowles, Mrs Camilla 101, 121, 123
  Camillagate conversations 3, 53–4, 158
  and Fred/Gladys bracelet 32
  Press treatment of 112
  and Prince Charles' choice of wife 34, 36
Paul VI, Pope 92
Pepys, Samuel 196
Petworth 36
Philip, HRH Prince, Duke of
  Edinburgh 60, 122, 168
  early life 119
  on the environment 154
  expression of views 73
  family tragedies 10–11
  hostility towards the Press 40, 106–7
  leads separate life from the Queen 116–17, 118–19, 133
  and 'modernising' of Royal Family 79
  and religion 152
  Rocco interview 117–18
  as royal spouse 131–3
  travelling expenses 173
  and Windsor fire 116
Phillips, Captain Mark 1, 94, 136, 138
Pius XII, Pope 92

Player, Lesley 104
Press Complaints Commission 97, 99
Princess's party 194–5
Private Eye 93, 98
Privy Purse 175, 183
Punch 175
Pyramids visit (1991) 101

Queen's Picture Gallery, London 180
Queen's Speech 58, 167

Reagan, Ronald 15
Rees-Mogg, Lord 204, 208
Reform Act (1867) 19
Regent's Park, London 180
Reynolds's Newspaper 84
Ribbentrop, Joachim Von 11n, 166
Richard III, King 198
Rocco, Fiametta 117, 132n, 133n
Roche, Frances 119
Roman Catholic Church 149, 150
Rose, Kenneth 8n, 111, 165n, 199n
Rothermere, Lord 99
Royal family (television film) 108–9, 189
Royal Lodge, Windsor 89–126
Royal Marriages Act 35
Royal Palaces Agency 182
Royal Parks 180
Royal Prerogative 133–4, 142, 163, 191–2

St James's Palace 182
St Paul's Cathedral 31, 32, 36, 37
Salazar, Dr Antonio de Oliviera 166
Salisbury, Lord 141
Sandringham House, Norfolk 31, 36, 83, 175, 178, 179, 183, 185, 197, 202
Sarah, Duchess of York 138
  attitude to marriage 123
  end of marriage to Prince Andrew 1, 136
  photograph scandal 1, 2–3, 60, 103–4, 158
  satirised 95
Save the Children Fund 80
Savoy, House of 197n
Scott, Selina 51–2